Recognition in the Bologna Process: policy development and the road to good practice

Andrejs Rauhvargers and Sjur Bergan (eds.)

Council of Europe Publishing

Cover design: Council of Europe Graphic Design Workshop
Layout: H. Mourreau/Heiligenberg

Council of Europe Publishing
F-67075 Strasbourg Cedex
http://book.coe.int

ISBN 978-92-871-6007-2
© Council of Europe, April 2006
Reprinted July 2008
Printed at the Council of Europe

Table of contents

Preface 5
Gabriele Mazza

A word from the editors 7
Andrejs Rauhvargers and Sjur Bergan

Recognition between Bologna and the European Higher Education
Area: status and overview 19
Andrejs Rauhvargers

The impact of emerging qualifications frameworks on recognition . . . 51
Stephen Adam

International recognition and quality assurance
– two priorities of the Bologna Process 63
Jindra Divis

Recognising learning outcomes 73
Norman Sharp

Recognition of credits – Achievements and challenges 81
Volker Gehmlich

Developments along subject lines and their impact on recognition . . 91
Julia González and Robert Waagenaar

Recognition for the labour market 103
Jindra Divis

The Bologna Process and recognition issues outside
the European Higher Education Area 115
E. Stephen Hunt

Programmes, providers and accreditors on the move:
implications for the recognition of qualifications 139
Jane Knight

The United States as a stakeholder in the Bologna Process 161
Timothy S. Thompson

Recognition 2010: opportunities from which we cannot run away ... 169
Sjur Bergan

Improving the recognition system of degrees and periods of studies:
conclusions and suggestions 183
Stephen Adam

Recommendations adopted by the conference 199

List of contributors 201

Preface

The Council of Europe Higher Education Series was launched in December 2004 with the aim of exploring higher education issues of concern to policy makers in ministries, at higher education institutions, in non-governmental organisations and elsewhere, and to make the Council of Europe's work in higher education policies more readily available to a broader public. With this book, within the space of approximately one year, we have already reached the fourth volume of the series.

The topic of this fourth volume is one that has been the most consistent feature of the Council of Europe higher education programme through the five decades of the European Cultural Convention: the recognition of qualifications. Ever since the first of the Council of Europe recognition conventions was adopted in 1953 – one year before the Cultural Convention – the Council of Europe has worked to make it easier for students and graduates to move across national borders without losing the real value of their qualifications. Both the Council of Europe's work and the nature of academic mobility have undergone profound changes during this time, and I firmly believe our activities have contributed to those developments.

The book you are about to read presents the most up-to-date overview of developments in the recognition field, and it also seeks to look ahead. The diversity of topics covered by the book is in itself a good indication of how far the recognition field has developed. Whereas it was once considered the preserve of highly technical specialists, recognition policies are now an essential part of overall higher education policy.

In part, this improved position is due to the Bologna Process aiming to establish a European Higher Education Area by 2010. Yet recognition policies are also one of the driving factors behind the Bologna Process, and the ultimate goal of the European Higher Education Area – to allow students, staff and holders of qualifications to move freely within as large an area of Europe as possible – cannot be attained without fair recognition of qualifications. It is with very good reason that the Council of Europe/UNESCO Recognition Convention was referred to in the Sorbonne Declaration of 1998, that ratification of the Convention was one of the elements of the stocktaking exercise carried out for the ministerial conference in Bergen in 2005, and that the Convention is so far the only legally binding text of the Bologna Process.

This book complements the third volume of the Higher Education Series, which is a compilation of the Convention and its subsidiary texts, with an introductory chapter that places the Convention in its proper context and provides a guide to understanding and using it.

I would like to express my appreciation of the work done by the editors of both volumes, Andrejs Rauhvargers and Sjur Bergan, to bring together both the essential standard-setting texts and the present collection of stimulating chapters on the main challenges in recognition policy. Together, volumes three and four of the Council of Europe Higher Education Series provide an excellent overview of the state of affairs in recognition policy as well as some stimulating thoughts on further developments.

Gabriele Mazza
Director of School, Out-of-School and Higher Education

A word from the editors

Andrejs Rauhvargers and Sjur Bergan

Improving the recognition of qualifications is essential to establishing a European Higher Education Area by 2010. In fact, the European Higher Education Area is unthinkable without widespread mobility of students, staff and holders of qualifications, and such mobility is difficult to imagine unless learners can have their qualifications recognised fairly and easily.

The book you are about to read seeks to provide a state of the art of recognition policies and their role in establishing the European Higher Education Area. It also aims to look ahead and to suggest policies and developments that will help make the European Higher Education Area a reality.

This book is based on presentations made at an official "Bologna seminar" on recognition – entitled Improving Recognition System of Degrees and Periods of Studies – organised in Riga in December 2004 by the Latvian authorities and the Council of Europe. All the authors have reviewed their articles after the conference, and the book offers a fairly complete overview of recognition issues on the eve of the ministerial conference of the Bologna Process held in Bergen in May 2005.[1]

As will be seen, the picture of recognition is a rich and composite one, and it illustrates the political importance of the recognition of qualifications, the diverse fields and purposes for which recognition is important and the variety of instruments used to further recognition. Thus, the contributions to this book cover topics as diverse as recognition and quality assurance, learning outcomes, recognition for the labour market, the impact of the new degree structures for the recognition of European degrees in North America and borderless or cross-border education.

To put the present in context, allow us to take a brief look at the recent past.

The recognition of qualifications has been one of the Council of Europe's main education activities for many years, and the Council's work has contributed to making the recognition of foreign qualifications much easier

---

1. See http://www.bologna-bergen2005.no/.

than it was a decade or two ago. The major recent milestones in this work are the Council of Europe/UNESCO Convention on the Recognition of Qualifications concerning Higher Education in the European Region (also referred to as the Council of Europe/UNESCO Recognition Convention and the Lisbon Recognition Convention), which was adopted in 1997, and the European Network of National Information Centres on academic recognition and mobility (ENIC Network).

By July 2005, the Council of Europe/UNESCO Recognition Convention had been ratified by 40 countries and signed by a further nine.[2] This convention is now the main standard for recognition of qualifications in Europe, and it is the only legally binding treaty that is a part of the Bologna Process. In addition, four subsidiary texts have so far been adopted under the Convention:

- the Recommendation on International Access Qualifications (1999);

- the Recommendation on Criteria and Procedures for the Assessment of Foreign Qualifications and Periods of Study (2001);

- the Code of Good Practice in the Provision of Transnational Education (2001);

- the Recommendation on the Recognition of Joint Degrees (2004).

It is worth noting that three of the four texts cover qualifications that either belong to several national systems or that belong to no such system.[3]

The ENIC Network was established in 1994, and it is now the main instrument for developing good recognition practice in Europe, in close co-operation with the NARIC[4] Network of the European Commission. The ENIC Network is made up of national information centres from some 50 countries in the European Region. Within their national context, each centre should be the first place that anyone would turn to for information on the higher education qualifications of the country in question or on the recognition of foreign qualifications in that country. In all but a

---

2. A continuously updated list of signatures and ratifications can be found at: http://conventions.coe.int/; search for ETS No.165.

3. The full text of the Council of Europe/UNESCO Recognition Convention as well as the subsidiary texts will be found in *Standards for Recognition: the Lisbon Recognition Convention and its Subsidiary Texts* (Strasbourg 2005: Council of Europe Publishing – Council of Europe Higher Education Series No. 3). The texts can also be found individually at the Council of Europe Higher Education website: http://www.coe.int/t/dg4/highereducation/Default_en.asp.

4. National Academic Recognition Information Centre.

few countries, the national information centres are just that: they provide information and often give a recommendation on recognition, but recognition cases are decided by other competent bodies. These would normally be a higher education institution if the purpose of the application is the pursuit of further study; a professional body or other competent professional recognition authority if the purpose is access to a regulated profession, such as medicine or architecture; or employers, if the purpose is access to the non-regulated part of the labour market. In the latter case, in many countries the national information centre may be able to issue a statement that, without being a formal recognition decision, describes the foreign qualification in relation to the education system of the country in which an individual seeks to obtain employment.

It is worth noting that both the Lisbon Recognition Convention and the ENIC Network are joint efforts by the Council of Europe and UNESCO, and that both organisations work closely with the European Commission in the area of recognition. The ENIC and NARIC Networks hold joint annual meetings and have issued joint statements on their contributions to the Bologna Process.[5]

As will be seen, both the Council of Europe/UNESCO Convention and the ENIC and NARIC Networks predate the Bologna Process, which was launched at a meeting of ministers of education from 29 European countries in Bologna in June 1999. Indeed, the Convention and the development of good recognition practice were among the developments that spurred the Bologna Process, and recognition policies have played an important role in it from the very beginning.

This is the second overview of recognition policies in the Bologna Process. The first was provided at a Bologna seminar organised in April 2002 in Lisbon by the Council of Europe and the Portuguese authorities, which also marked the fifth anniversary of the adoption of the Lisbon Recognition Convention.[6]

Several important developments have taken place since 2002, and Andrejs Rauhvargers provides an extensive overview of these. In his chapter it is emphasised that these developments take place at national as well as international level, and that an important feature of the Bologna Process is in fact that overall policy goals are agreed at international level

---

5. Further information on the ENIC and NARIC Networks may be found at: http://www.enic-naric.net.
6. The 2002 conference gave rise to Sjur Bergan (ed.): *Recognition Issues in the Bologna Process* (Strasbourg 2003: Council of Europe Publishing).

but implemented nationally, whether through national legislation and policies or at higher education institutions. This "double framework" gave rise to one of the most important recommendations from the conference, which was also included in the Bergen Communiqué, in which ministers committed themselves to ensuring the full implementation of the Council of Europe/UNESCO Convention and to incorporating these principles into national legislation as appropriate.

A particularly striking feature of the developments since 2002 is the development of qualifications frameworks. These are descriptions of all qualifications in a given education system, and they emphasise what learners know and can do on the basis of given qualifications – in other words, learning outcomes – as well as how learners can move between various qualifications – in other words, how the qualifications within a given system interlink. Stephen Adam discusses the impact of qualifications frameworks on recognition. Among other things, he points out that while qualifications frameworks will improve transparency, facilitate comparisons and reduce the time credential evaluators spend on each recognition case, qualifications frameworks are no "magic wand" that will make recognition automatic. Much work needs to be done to develop national frameworks, which so far exist in only a handful of countries. We would also add that making full use of qualifications frameworks will also require developing attitudes among credential evaluators.

Quality assurance is one of the most hotly discussed areas of higher education policy in Europe today and, with recognition and the reform of the degree structure, one of the three areas singled out for stocktaking prior to the Bergen conference.[7] Jindra Divis points out that while accountability, protection of the public interest and quality improvement are the most frequently stated arguments for quality assurance, these are mainly national goals. At international level, the ultimate goal of quality assurance is to facilitate the recognition of qualifications. Recognition of individual qualifications assumes knowledge of the education system and institution or programme from which the qualifications stem, since otherwise a credential evaluator would be unable to assess the real quality of a qualification. However, while quality assurance is an important element in a recognition decision, this decision also has to take into account other elements, and it will ultimately seek to assess learning outcomes. It is important that quality assurance agencies provide information in such a

---

7. The stocktaking report submitted to the Bergen conference may be found at: http://www.bologna-bergen2005.no/Bergen/050509_Stocktaking.pdf.

way that this information is easily accessible to credential evaluators, and it is equally important that credential evaluators specify their need for information. Jindra Divis describes a number of initiatives that are under way to improve co-operation between the quality assurance and recognition communities.

Norman Sharp's chapter on recognising learning outcomes sets out to define – and also "demystify" – this commonly used but sometimes inadequately understood concept. Norman Sharp points out that an emphasis on learning outcomes helps academic staff specify the objectives of their courses, and it helps students have realistic expectations of a given course or programme and also to assess whether an interesting sounding programme will actually meet their needs. Specifying learning outcomes is essential to achieving the mobility and flexibility that are cornerstones of the Bologna Process, and it is also of great importance to the recognition of prior learning. The alternative to developing learning outcomes is to continue to rely on the formal characteristics of study programmes, such as the length of study. That, however, would not be much better than judging a book by the design of its cover or the number of pages.

Credits are an important instrument in measuring learning achievements and in allowing these achievements to be transferred from one institution or system to another. In the time since the 1999 Bologna conference, they have largely replaced the more diffuse concept of "time of study" as the measure of student workload, and they greatly facilitate the transfer and recognition of units below degree level – what are often referred to as periods of study. Volker Gehmlich gives close consideration to the European Credit Transfer System (ECTS), which is now to all intents and purposes the only system used for credit transfer at European level. It is now being developed to facilitate not only credit transfer, but also credit accumulation. Volker Gehmlich examines the ECTS in relation to four factors:

1. Suitability – is ECTS fit for purpose?

2. Acceptability – is ECTS fit for stakeholders?

3. Feasibility – is ECTS fit to live?

4. Sustainability – is ECTS fit for life?

He compares the ECTS to a currency system and points out that, like a common currency, the ECTS as the credit transfer and accumulation system of the European Higher Education Area requires trust and adherence to "stability criteria" such as transparency and tuned structures, processes and outcomes.

11

Current thinking about recognition has also been refined through the Tuning project,[8] which is financed by the European Commission and carried out by a consortium co-ordinated by the Universities of Deusto and Groningen. The project is now in its third phase. In their chapter, the Tuning co-ordinators, Julia González and Robert Wagenaar, describe the work of the Tuning Project to develop descriptions of learning outcomes in specific subject areas. The first phase of the Tuning Project encompassed educational sciences, mathematics, business, history, geology, physics and chemistry, while the second phase also included nursing and European Studies. The rationale for including an additional two subject areas in the second phase was to extend the project to a regulated as well as a multidisciplinary field of studies. Within each subject area, the project focused on degree profiles, which guide the definition of learning outcomes and competencies. These are divided into subject specific learning outcomes and competencies, which are specific to, for example, history or chemistry, and transversal learning outcomes and competencies that are common to all or most forms of higher education. Examples of the latter are the ability to reason in abstract terms, to solve problems and to explain issues in terms that make them understandable to non-subject specialists.

For most students, one important reason for undertaking higher education is to improve opportunities for interesting and rewarding employment. At the same time, modern, complex societies increasingly need a large number of highly educated people. Increasingly, highly educated people seek employment not only in their countries of origin, but also in other parts of Europe. Therefore, recognition for the labour market is a key issue, as is borne out by Jindra Divis's second chapter in this volume. While academic recognition refers to the recognition of qualifications for the purpose of further study, professional recognition refers to the recognition of qualifications with a view to entering the labour market. The term "professional recognition" is most commonly used with respect to access to regulated professions (typical examples of which are medicine, law and architecture), but in many cases, applicants need recognition of their foreign qualifications to obtain employment in the non-regulated part of the labour market. In these cases, recognition is in fact carried out by prospective employers, but ENICs/NARICs could play an important role in advising employers about foreign qualifications. Some ENICs/NARICs have already established contacts with employers and their organisations, and professional recognition will be an increasingly important task for ENICs/NARICs in

---

8. Tuning Educational Structures in Europe:
http://www.relint.deusto.es/TuningProject/index.htm or
http://tuning.unideusto.org/tuningeu/

the years to come. The increased emphasis on recognition of learning outcomes and assessment of competencies, regardless of the learning path the applicant has followed, will also play an important role in improving recognition for the labour market.

So far, most of the discussions around the Bologna Process have focused on internal aspects, by which we mean the need for reform of higher education in Europe and the effect these reforms are expected to have within the European Higher Education Area. It was perhaps natural that launching and implementing such a broad reform process would lead to an amount of navel-gazing, at least in its early stages. Nevertheless, the Bologna Process also has serious implications for other regions of the world and for Europe's relations with these regions.

One of the most serious concerns is how the new style "Bologna degrees" will be recognised in other parts of the world.[9] E. Stephen Hunt points out that the "external dimension" has been present in the Bologna Process from the very beginning, since the Process was in part designed to meet the challenge to European higher education from other parts of the world, in particular North America and Australia, yet most actors in the Bologna Process have until very recently been reluctant to acknowledge this dimension. Therefore, they have also failed to recognise early signals about how important partners outside Europe would react to some of the proposed reforms, in particular the move towards a first degree based on 180 ECTS credits. Only a meaningful dialogue based on an understanding of the various higher education systems, including the considerable variety between European systems and what are commonly but erroneously referred to as "Anglo-Saxon" systems as well as within the US higher education system can bring us closer to fair mutual recognition. This requires addressing technical issues like credit calculation and degree systems, but it also requires considering broader issues such as US-European interchange and trade in higher education. Not least, policy makers and recognition specialists in all parts of the world must recognise that reforms and changes have not abolished the need for recognition and quality assurance professionals, but have in fact increased the complexity and scope of their work. They must also show due respect for how systems legitimately differ. We can at least take some heart from one important development after E. Stephen Hunt's chapter

---

9. For a broad discussion of the so-called "external dimension of the Bologna Process, see Franziska Muche (ed.): *Opening Up to the Wider World: the External Dimension of the Bologna Process* (Bonn 2005: Lemmens Verlags- und Medieengesellschaft/ACA Papers on international co-operation in education).

was written: the Bergen Ministerial meeting put the relationship between the European Higher Education Area and the rest of the world squarely on the agenda of the Bologna Process as part of the work programme for 2005-2007.

The Bologna Process addresses the reform of national higher education systems in Europe, and credential evaluators as well as policy makers have been used to dealing mostly with qualifications issued by institutions and programmes that belong to a national system. Increasingly, however, they are faced with higher education provision that has few or no ties to any national system. Jane Knight outlines the rapid growth of such provision, which was initially referred to as transnational, but is now most frequently termed cross-border or even borderless higher education. She also shows the complexity of cross-border education, a common feature of which is, however, that it seeks to replace traditional student mobility with the physical or virtual mobility of higher education provision. In some cases, higher education programmes "move" through a main provider entering into co-operation agreement with local agents, whereas in other cases local partners are absent.

The vast diversity of provision is a challenge to recognition specialists in itself, since proper consideration of qualifications earned across borders requires knowledge of a very broad range of providers and types of programmes. The challenge is greatly compounded by the fact that many cross-border providers operate for a brief period of time and that they are, for the most part, not subject to external quality assurance. While closing one's eyes to the emergence of this type of higher education provision and refusing recognition to any qualification that does not stem from a national education system is not a viable solution and would discriminate against holders of qualifications from bona fide cross-border education, the lack of objective, verifiable information is a serious issue. Some international initiatives have been taken to address this issue. An early initiative was the UNESCO/Council of Europe Code of Good Practice in the Provision of Transnational Education, which was adopted as a subsidiary text to the Lisbon Recognition Convention in 1999. Currently, UNESCO and the OECD are in the process of adopting Guidelines for Quality Provision in Cross-border Higher Education, and UNESCO has also launched a revision of at least some of its regional conventions on the model of the Lisbon Convention.

Timothy S. Thompson underscores that one important reason why US higher education and research has been vibrant is that the US system has been very open to students and researchers from other parts of the world.

However, there are currently signs that many foreigners are now also looking elsewhere for quality education, and one of the challenges for US – as well as for European – higher education will be to keep its doors open. In this respect, US higher education is likely to see itself as a stakeholder in the Bologna Process. Timothy Thompson outlines the main characteristics of the US higher education system and describes the National Council on the Evaluation of Foreign Credentials. Owing to the absence of a government role or competence in the recognition of foreign qualifications in the US, the National Council plays a unique role as the only inter-associational body in the United States offering standards for interpreting foreign educational credentials and for the purpose of assisting educational institutions in admitting and placing students primarily in academic programmes of study. These standards are advisory rather than compulsory, and there are many actors in the field, including private assessment services and the American Association of Collegiate Registrars and Admission Officers (AACRAO). This diversity, which can be confusing to outsiders, sometimes leads to different assessments of similar degrees, and this is also likely to be the case for the recognition of new "Bologna degrees". Even if Europeans may find it difficult to identify the most suitable partners for dialogue with the United States, such dialogue is essential to further mutual recognition between US institutions and those of the European Higher Education Area.

2010 is the target date for establishing the European Higher Education Area, and it therefore seemed imperative that the book include a reflection on the recognition issues that will be most pertinent in this context. Sjur Bergan points out that it is sometimes difficult to distinguish predictions – indications of what is likely to happen – from our own desires for the future – what we would like to see happen. Predictions are nevertheless useful, not least because they may help us identify likely developments as well as what action we might take to help those developments go in the direction we would like. The legal framework for recognition is now largely in place, not least thanks to the Lisbon Recognition Convention and its subsidiary texts, and one of the main challenges will therefore lie in the implementation of the existing legal framework rather than in developing a new one. It should nevertheless be pointed out that, as recognised by the ministers in Bergen, many national legal frameworks may still have to be amended to take account of international developments and countries' obligations under the Lisbon Recognition Convention. It should also be remembered that laws are only effective if they are implemented and enforced, and that enforcement is mostly linked to national authorities, national territories and national systems.

This is not to say that the international legal framework is worthless or ineffective, but rather to say that the Council of Europe/UNESCO Convention as well as other legal and standard-setting texts have another important function: they are also guides to good practice. Therefore, the interpretation of legislation and actual recognition practice are of paramount importance. There has already been a very significant development from what is often referred to as "equivalence" to "recognition", in other words from a very detailed comparison of curricula and structures to a broader view. Recognition is essentially about determining whether applicants' learning achievements are such that they are likely to succeed in activities they want to undertake on the basis of their qualifications, whether for further study or in the labour market. Therefore, we need to assess what applicants know and can do rather than the structures and procedures through which they have obtained their qualifications.

Ultimately, one of the main challenges for the recognition community will be to develop the attitudes of recognition specialists from one of detailed comparison to one of broad considerations of outcomes, from one of looking for problems to one of looking for solutions. Granting fair recognition does not mean that one should recognise all qualifications regardless of their merits, but it does mean that one should look at their real merits and give them due recognition for these. This also applies to the recognition of cross-border and non-traditional qualifications, and it is essential to the recognition of European qualifications outside the European Higher Education Area. In this context, however, Europeans must consider non-European qualifications with the same openness with which we expect non-Europeans to assess our own qualifications, and we must be as willing to assess learning outcomes rather than formal procedures. Recognition is not a one-way street, and it is highly dependent on providing accurate and readily understandable information. The information strategy adopted by the ENIC and NARIC Networks in 2004 is an important step in this direction, and it will hopefully help bring about a future in which credential evaluators should spend less time assessing clear-cut cases, and where they will have more time to devote to complicated cases; the ones that truly require the sustained attention of specialists with a good knowledge of various education systems and above all with a solid knowledge of the principles of recognition and the ability to apply those principles to individual cases.

In his concluding chapter, Stephen Adam summarises the issues raised at the conference. His chapter also leads up to the recommendations adopted. He maintains that the Bologna Process has given a sharp boost to every aspect of the recognition field. This positive progress needs to be developed by making existing tools work better, fully implementing the Lisbon Recognition Convention and widening knowledge of good practice at all levels – local, regional, national and international. Stephen Adam likens the recognition field to an iceberg, where the visible parts and procedures are effective and proven to work and the problem lies with the submerged nine-tenths. As editors of the present volume, we would in particular like to underscore some of Stephen Adam's conclusions, which provide a comprehensive overview of the main challenges facing both recognition specialists and higher education policy makers as we will move from a new order in the making to what will hopefully be an improved world for students, staff and holders of qualifications, as well as for European societies as large. Meeting these challenges will to a large extent determine whether we will meet our stated goal of moving from the Bologna Process to the European Higher Education Area by 2010.

Once established, the European Higher Education Area will continue to develop. In this case, as in many others, the alternative to further development will be stagnation and failure. The European Higher Education Area will not be the best of all possible worlds, nor will it be a paradise lost. However, we are optimistic that the European Higher Education Area will be a framework within which large numbers of students and staff will be partners in quality higher education and research for which their own geographic or social origin or the geographic location of their higher education will be considerably less important than it is today. We are also convinced that improving the recognition of qualifications is a key factor in its success or failure, and we are optimistic that what is often loosely referred to as the "recognition community" will rise to the challenge. We believe that the chapters in this book justify our optimism, and we hope our readers will reach the same conclusion.

This book is the fruit of the work of several authors. They have all revised their contributions to the conference, and we would like to thank them all for their good work and for being open to our editorial suggestions. Without such a representative selection of authors, providing a "state of the art" as well as well-founded reflections on the challenges ahead would have been much more difficult, and it would not have been possible to attain the variety of viewpoints represented. We would also like to thank Sophie Ashmore of the Council of Europe's Higher Education and Research Division for her help with the manuscript and Council of Europe Publishing for all their assistance.

Recognition between Bologna and the European Higher Education Area: status and overview

Andrejs Rauhvargers

Setting the scene

Recognition of qualifications with a view to the creation of a European Higher Education Area

Recognition of qualifications[10] is an important component of the whole development towards the European Higher Education Area. One can argue that improving recognition of qualifications earned in one of the Bologna Process countries across all other Bologna Process countries is a necessary precondition for establishing the European Higher Education Area.

There are several goals that can only be reached if proper recognition of qualifications between states and education systems is ensured. Recognition of qualifications is a precondition to ensuring practical possibilities for free movement of persons, including free flow of the labour force. In addition, the goal of increasing competitiveness of European higher education on a world scale can only be reached if qualifications awarded by European higher education institutions are recognised outside Europe – and this can hardly be the case if they are not recognised in other European countries.

The adoption of the Lisbon Recognition Convention [1], as acknowledged in the Sorbonne declaration [2] of 1998, was an achievement to build on:

> "The [Lisbon Recognition] Convention set a number of basic requirements and acknowledged that individual countries could engage in an even more constructive scheme. Standing by these conclusions, one can build on them and go further."

---

10. The author has chosen to use "qualifications" as the generic term used in the Lisbon Recognition Convention in order to cover all kinds of educational credentials: degrees, diplomas, certificates, and so on.

The overall relevance of recognition to the main action lines of the Bologna Declaration on the European Higher Education Area [3] can be summarised as follows:

– Adoption of a system of easily readable and comparable degrees. Without improved recognition procedures, citizens will not be able to use their qualifications, competencies and skills throughout the European Higher Education Area, and such a system will not bring the benefits which are expected.

– Adoption of a system essentially based on two main cycles. Given the diversity of the academic offer currently available across Europe, recognition issues will be essential in helping clarify the adaptation of undergraduate/postgraduate structures, and in facilitating different orientations and profiles of study programmes.

– Promotion of mobility. This goal is considered by ministers to be of utmost importance, and the full application of the provisions of the Lisbon Recognition Convention would be a significant step forward in pursuing the removal of all obstacles to the free movement of students, teachers, researchers and administrative staff.

– Promotion of European co-operation in quality assurance. The seminar underlined the necessary links between quality assurance and recognition, and the need for closer co-operation between actors in these two fields, at institutional, national and European levels.

– Promotion of the European dimension in higher education. The fair recognition of qualifications can play an important facilitating role in the development of partnerships and joint degrees between institutions in different countries.

– Lifelong learning. Prior learning assessment and recognition and the assessment of non-traditional qualifications are essential in facilitating lifelong learning opportunities and strategies.

– Promotion of the attractiveness of the European Higher Education Area. Recognition issues are an integral element of ensuring the enhanced attractiveness of European higher education to students from Europe and other parts of the world. [4]

In their Berlin Communiqué of 19 September 2003 on "Realising the European Higher Education Area" [5] the European ministers responsible for higher education "commit[ted] themselves to intermediate priorities for the next two years[:] ... to promote effective quality assurance systems, to step up effective use of the system based on two cycles and to improve the recognition system of degrees and periods of studies". To ensure that these priority issues were accordingly addressed, the ministers charged the intergovernmental Bologna Follow-up Group with organising a stocktaking process and preparing reports on progress in these three priority areas for their summit in 2005.

Ministers also underlined the importance of the Lisbon Recognition Convention, which should be ratified by all countries participating in the Bologna Process, and called on the ENIC[11] and NARIC[12] Networks and the competent national authorities to further the implementation of the Convention.

Acknowledging that more transparency and relevant information was needed, they also set the objective that every student graduating from 2005 should receive the Joint European Diploma Supplement automatically and free of charge.

The Berlin Communiqué also addresses two more specific recognition issues. Firstly, the ministers agreed to take steps at national level to remove legal obstacles to the establishment and recognition of joint degrees and to support adequate quality assurance of curricula leading to joint degrees. Secondly, when addressing the need to make lifelong learning a reality, ministers urged higher education institutions and all concerned to enhance the possibilities for lifelong learning at higher education level, including the recognition of prior learning.

Definitions regarding recognition

Recognition issues have come under focus in the Bologna Process discussions and these discussions have been ongoing among a wide range of stakeholders: policy makers, higher education staff, students, employers, different higher education-related institutions, and society at large. These discussions have sometimes been confusing because different discussion partners have had in mind different definitions of the term "recognition".

While there may be other ways in which the term "recognition" is used,[13] for the purposes of this chapter the most important ones are the following:

11. ENIC: Council of Europe/UNESCO European Network of Information Centres for recognition and mobility.
12. NARIC: EU network of National Academic Recognition Information Centres.
13. For example, recognition of a programme by a national or international professional association leading to admission of graduates to pursuit of particular profession(s), recognition of an institution or programme by a kind of international body/association of a certain type of institutions or programmes, and so on.

Recognition of a higher education institution. As a precondition to international recognition, an institution should first be recognised nationally. In the fairly recent past, the national systems for quality assurance were just emerging. Thus, when countries were asked to supply information regarding nationally recognised institutions, compiling such lists could be a rather arbitrary procedure. The appearance of new types of higher education provision has changed the situation. Nowadays lists of nationally recognised institutions are more and more often compiled on the basis of (at least some kind of) quality assessment, ranging from relatively "soft" procedures to national accreditation.

Recognition of a higher education programme – with the consequence that the credentials issued are nationally recognised. National recognition of the institution alone does not automatically imply national recognition of all its programmes and, as a consequence, the qualifications awarded. In a number of European countries, some of the programmes run by recognised institutions may not lead to nationally recognised qualifications. In such cases institutions often issue credentials "in their own name" and these qualifications usually have a different status from the "national" qualifications, which no doubt makes international recognition more difficult.

Recognition of an individual qualification nationally. If both the institution and the programme in question are recognised nationally, it normally follows that the qualification awarded is nationally recognised, in other words that the qualification is normally valid for all administrative purposes, and that other higher education institutions will consider the holder for admission to the next stage of studies. It will also mean eligibility for jobs in non-regulated professions or to those jobs for which there is a general requirement of holding a qualification of a certain level.

Recognition of an individual qualification abroad. It is this meaning of the term "recognition" that is relevant and crucial for European co-operation and for the goals of the Bologna Process – ensuring that qualifications earned in one part of the European Higher Education Area are valid for further studies, and also for employment in other parts of the area.

Taking into account the wide European diversity and encompassing the aim of cross-border mobility for both study and employment purposes, a purely formal acknowledgement of foreign credentials is not sufficient. The real task of credential evaluators is to assess the foreign qualification with a view to finding the right path for further studies or employment in the host country.

Because of the reasons discussed above, "recognition" in this chapter will be understood as the assessment of a foreign qualification with a view to finding ways for its application for further studies and/or employment in the host country.

The international framework

According to purpose, recognition may be divided into two types: academic recognition for further studies and professional recognition for employment purposes.

The aspect of professional recognition which deals with regulated professions has specific legislation in the EU and EEA: the directives on professional recognition. Following the EU's enlargement on 1 May 2004, the EU directives for professional recognition will cover 29 of the 40 countries involved in the Bologna Process. To date, the EU system for professional recognition consists of: sectoral directives dealing specifically with recognition in particular professions – those of medical doctor, dentist, nurse responsible for general care, midwife, pharmacist, veterinary surgeon, architect and lawyer; and of general systems directives, dealing with all other regulated professions. Sectoral directives stipulate harmonisation of education for the particular profession across the EU/EEA and further automatic recognition between the member states. The principle underlying the general system is that a qualification of a professional[14] from another member state will be recognised unless there are *substantial differences* in education and training. A proposal for a new directive that will join both systems together and merge all the existing professional recognition directives into a single text but will not change the basic principles is currently in the process of adoption by the European Parliament.

The main legal instrument for academic recognition in the European Region is the Council of Europe/UNESCO *Convention on the Recognition of Qualifications Concerning Higher Education* (ETS No. 165) [1], adopted in Lisbon on 11 April 1997 (also referred to as the Lisbon Recognition Convention).

---

14. While the term "recognition of diplomas" is used in the directives, the definition of "diploma" also includes all the additional training, practical placements and other requirements that a holder of an educational qualification has to fulfil before being granted the right to practise the profession independently. See Directive 89/48/EEC, Article 1:
http://europa.eu.int/smartapi/cgi/sga_doc?smartapi!celexapi!prod!CELEXnumdoc&lg= EN&numdoc=31989L0048&model=guichett

Although the main field of application of the Lisbon Recognition Convention is academic recognition, the Convention can also be, and increasingly is, of use for cases of recognition concerning the non-regulated part of the labour market. In these cases no official recognition is formally required. However, when considering a candidate with a foreign qualification, employers often wish to know to which of the qualifications of their country the foreign one can be compared. In such cases candidates may seek a statement of academic recognition. The situation is similar in those cases when access to a profession requires a certain level of education without specifying the field.

The Explanatory report on Article VI.3 says, among other things:

> "... this Article concerns the recognition, for employment purposes, of the knowledge and skills certified by a higher education qualification issued in another Party. The recognition of other components of a qualification, such as practice periods ..., are not covered by this Article, nor does this Article in any way affect national laws and regulations on the exercise of professional activities or gainful employment, as the case may be."

The most important principles of the Lisbon Recognition Convention are the following:

Right to a fair assessment of foreign qualifications. The Lisbon Recognition Convention was the first international legal instrument in which this right was laid down. Such a right might sound like a very basic issue. However, before the adoption of the Lisbon Recognition Convention, holders of foreign qualifications sometimes found that their credentials were simply not accepted for evaluation, thus possibly hinting at an unwillingness to recognise a foreign qualification or a lack of knowledge of the education system from which the foreign qualification originated.

Recognition if no substantial differences are evident. The Lisbon Recognition Convention replaced seeking full "equivalence" of the foreign qualification to the host country's one by recognition of the foreign qualification if there are no substantial differences with the host country's qualification to which the foreign qualification is being compared.

The Convention also states that should the host country authorities consider non-recognition, it is their duty to demonstrate that the differences are substantial.

Mutual trust and provision of information. Recognition under the Lisbon Convention is based upon mutual trust and provision of information between the higher education systems of the States Parties to the Convention. For this reason the Parties have an obligation both to compile and publish lists of their recognised institutions and programmes and to provide information regarding qualifications, programmes and institutions. While the term "quality assurance" is not used in this context in the Convention, it would seem difficult to argue, in today's context, that information on the institutions and programmes that make up a national higher education system could be provided without reference to quality assurance.

The Council of Europe/UNESCO Recommendation on Criteria and Procedures for the Assessment of Foreign Qualifications was adopted by the Intergovernmental Committee of the Lisbon Recognition Convention on 4 June 2001. The recommendation is a step forward from the Lisbon Convention itself. It was originally planned to help to ensure that similar recognition cases will be considered in reasonably similar ways throughout the European region. Drafting of the Recommendation was in progress when the Bologna Declaration was signed, which also made it possible to draw on the analysis of the recognition issues made by the Bologna Process [6, 7] and to adapt the implementation of the Convention accordingly:

–   The recommendation demonstrates that the principles of the Convention can also be applied in cases of recognition concerning the non-regulated part of the labour market.

–   The recommendation extends recognition to qualifications awarded after completion of transnational education that complies with the Code of Good Practice in the Provision of Transnational Education.[15]

–   The recommendation shifts the focus of credential evaluation from input characteristics of the programmes – curriculum contents, course programmes, duration, textbooks covered, and so on – to the learning outcomes and competencies.

–   It is underlined that, when analysing differences, the purpose for which recognition of the foreign qualification is sought should be kept in mind. Given the wide diversity of programmes and qualifications in Europe, any foreign qualification will always have differences with the one it is being compared to. The recommendation calls for a positive attitude towards foreign qualifications, always asking the question of whether the differences really are so great that it is impossible to use the foreign qualification for the purpose for

---

15. The issue of recognition of transnational education qualifications is discussed in greater detail below.

which recognition is sought, and if they are, whether it is possible to grant at least alternative or partial recognition.

–   Through shifting the focus from input characteristics to learning outcomes, the recommendation also facilitates recognition of lifelong learning or other non-traditional qualifications.

–   The recommendation underlines that if a competent authority finds that it cannot grant full recognition of a foreign qualification, it should consider granting partial recognition.

The recommendation neither introduces anything revolutionary or totally alien to the recognition community, nor does it say that recognition should always be granted. Rather, it codifies established best practice among credential evaluators and builds on this practice in suggesting further improvements.

The Recommendation for the Recognition of International Access Qualifications [8] was adopted in 1999. This document specifically addresses international secondary school leaving certificates such as the International Baccalaureate, the European Baccalaureate and others.

The Code of Good Practice for the Provision of Transnational Education, adopted in 2001, and the Recommendation on the Recognition of Joint Degrees, adopted in 2004, address important relatively new recognition issues and are therefore discussed separately below.

Implementation of the legal framework for recognition

Existence of a relevant legal framework for recognition is a necessary precondition for solving the recognition problems across the European Higher Education Area, but another precondition is its proper implementation, both nationally and internationally.

The international level

Signatures and ratifications of the Convention

The first step of improving recognition in the European Higher Education Area is signature and ratification of the Convention by all the countries concerned. This need was specifically underlined in the Berlin Communiqué adopted by the ministers [5]. The ministerial call has been heard: although the number of signatures and ratifications of the Lisbon Convention was already quite impressive before the Berlin conference, five more Bologna Process countries have ratified the Convention since September 2003. The total number of ratifications as of 10 March 2006 is 41, of which 33 concern countries participating in the Bologna Process.

The two countries that have so far applied for accession to the Bologna Process prior to the Bergen ministerial conference (19 and 20 May 2005) – Moldova and Ukraine – have both ratified the Convention.

The area covered by the Lisbon Recognition Convention is wider than the "Bologna" group of countries and also wider than geographical Europe. Australia, Canada, USA, Israel and certain other countries belonging to the European region as defined by UNESCO have also signed the Convention. This is of considerable importance to the external dimension of the European Higher Education Area, as it stimulates recognition between European countries and other parts of the world.

Five out of the forty-five "Bologna" countries – Belgium, Germany, Italy, the Netherlands and Turkey – have signed the Convention and are in the process of ratification, but another three countries – Andorra, Greece and Spain – have so far neither signed nor ratified it. Some of these countries are meanwhile trying to follow its principles in practice. As recognition is set as a priority issue of the Bologna Process for the forthcoming period until May 2007, it is likely that some more signatures and ratifications may follow before the time of the stocktaking exercise for the London ministerial conference.

European recognition networks

As stated on page 62 of the *Trends 2003* report, the recognition networks ENIC and NARIC serve as the main agent for the implementation of the Lisbon Convention and, more generally, for improved recognition within Europe [9]. The Lisbon Recognition Convention stipulates that each State Party to the Convention is to establish an information centre for academic recognition and that the national centres together are to form the ENIC Network.

A narrower group of national centres within the EU/EEA form the NARIC network, which covers specific tasks within the EU, including the functioning of contact points for professional recognition in the EU and EEA. Thus, the national centres of the enlarged EU plus EEA countries participate in both Networks.

Analysing recognition issues and preparing new international legislation. The ENIC and NARIC Networks have established a number of ad hoc working groups which have studied urgent recognition issues and suggested measures to develop the recognition system in Europe, such as the working group that developed the format of the joint European Diploma Supplement, the one on transnational education, recognition criteria and procedures and the group on recognition issues in the Bologna

27

Process. The latter came up with a report on *Recognition Issues in the Bologna Process* [6] that serves as guidelines for further improvement of the recognition system.

The networks have drafted international legal documents supplementing the Lisbon Convention: the Recommendation on Criteria and Procedures for the Assessment of Foreign Qualifications [10] and the Code of Good Practice in the Provision of Transnational Education [11] (both adopted in June 2001). In view of the need to improve recognition of joint degrees, the networks prepared a Recommendation for the Recognition of Joint Degrees [12] that was adopted in June 2004.

International information exchange. Fulfilling the designated task of providing information on their own higher education systems, the networks' member centres supply recognition-related information upon the request of other centres in their everyday work. ENIC/NARIC centres efficiently supply each other with information on particular qualifications or the status of a higher education institution/programme through the ENIC/NARIC listserver. Also, using the ENIC/NARIC website[16] one can easily find the links to the national ENIC/NARIC centres, most of which contain descriptions of their countries' higher education systems and other relevant information concerning recognition.

The national level

One very positive aspect in this regard is that as shown in the *Trends 2003* report (p. 66) [9], more and more countries have introduced the Diploma Supplement. The requirement of the European ministers that the Diploma Supplement should be issued automatically to every graduate by 2005 will speed this aspect up even more. However, it should be noted that issuing Diploma Supplements is helping countries' own qualifications to be recognised abroad. Developments are not so quick when it comes to amending national legislation with a view to ensuring the fair recognition of foreign qualifications.

National legal issues

Ratification of the Lisbon Convention is not enough if the principles of the Convention are not transposed into the national legislation and national procedures remain unchanged. There are several countries in Europe which, while having signed and ratified the Lisbon Convention, have followed a national procedure of "nostrification". Analysis of the

---

16. http://www.enic-naric.net

results of a Council of Europe survey on implementation of the Lisbon recognition convention [13] shows that (op.cit.):

"...answers deal with recognition practice and attitudes toward recognition. They reveal a difference between those [countries] who primarily consider formal recognition criteria and seek to establish as close a resemblance as possible between foreign qualifications and those of the home country and those that move in the direction of seeking to assess learning outcomes. In short-hand, and at the risk of oversimplification, these different approaches may be termed 'equivalence' vs. 'recognition'."

It also leads to a conclusion that:

"some countries have yet to implement the main principles of the Lisbon Recognition Convention, which point in the direction of an overall assessment of the level and profile of a qualification rather than a detailed comparison of contents" [13].

National setting and procedures for recognition

At national level, decisions on recognition are usually taken either by higher education institutions (for academic purposes), by employers (for employment purposes in the non-regulated part of the labour market) and by professional bodies or other nationally appointed competent authorities (for the pursuit of regulated professions). The above survey also shows that the national situation of the ENIC/NARIC centres may differ. In most countries the main expertise and knowledge of foreign educational systems is concentrated within the ENIC/NARIC centres. These centres evaluate credentials and give advice to the different types of decision-making bodies. Co-operation may be organised in different ways: in some countries the higher education institutions only apply to the ENIC/NARIC centres for advice in more complicated cases, in others every holder of a foreign qualification has to receive a statement from an ENIC/NARIC centre. It is quite common practice that the decision-making bodies trust the expertise of the ENIC/NARIC centre and follow its advice, that is in practice the statement by the recognition centre is the decision.

While this is the practical setting in a good number of European countries, in which the ENIC/NARIC centres are well-equipped and reasonably well-staffed bodies capable of carrying out all their tasks (international and national information exchange, evaluation of individual credentials, consultancy for all stakeholders, and so on), in some others the "recognition information centre" may be just a single ministry employee appointed as a national contact point, and this person may have several other duties in parallel. In the latter case, the ENIC/NARIC usually serves just as an information provider and network member (in many cases giving a valuable input into international developments), but it does not deal with recognition of individual qualifications or individual information requests at all – which would also mean that in these countries the assessment of foreign qualifications by numerous individual higher education institutions will take place in an unco-ordinated way, and hence there is little chance that the procedures and criteria will be similar across the country.

Institutional recognition procedures – are they sufficiently developed?

Given that higher education institutions are the final instances, which decide upon recognition for further studies, the awareness of institutions about the principles of international legislation on recognition and the existence of institutional policies and procedures for recognition are of crucial importance for the practical implementation of the international legal framework. What is the situation in practice? To quote the *Trends 2003* report, "it is clear that there is room for improvement, in particular in certain countries" [9].

According to the *Trends 2003* report, when asked about the awareness of the provisions of the Lisbon Convention within their countries, almost 60%[17] of heads of higher education institutions thought that their staff were either "not very aware" or "almost completely unaware". About half of student organisations thought the same about their institutions.

As regards institutional procedures for recognition, according to the *Trends 2003* report (op.cit.), the answers to the questionnaire demonstrated that the weakest point seems to be institutional procedures for recognition of foreign degrees: only 58% of higher education institutions declared they had an institution-wide procedure for this issue, ranging from as many as 83% down to 13% in different countries. As for the students, more than a third thought their institutions had no institution-wide recognition policy but were taking decisions on a case-by-case basis.

As for the recognition of study periods taken abroad, the situation is better – around 82% of institutions have procedures for recognition of study abroad, which is probably related to the use of ECTS in exchanges under the Socrates-Erasmus programme. Still, there seems to be evidence of cases where even after a study period abroad agreed in advance under the Erasmus programme, the credits earned abroad are scrupulously

---

17. Data here and subsequently in this chapter are taken from the *Trends 2003* report.

assessed in an attempt to seek full concordance with the home courses to be replaced by these credits.

In the vast majority of countries higher education institutions can receive qualified consultancy and assistance in recognition matters from their national ENIC/NARIC centres, but are the higher education institutions seeking that assistance? The *Trends 2003* survey results show that "only 20% of the higher education institutions (27.5% of universities) report a *close* co-operation with their NARIC/ENIC. 24% regard their co-operation as *limited* and almost one quarter indicated that there is *no co-operation at all*".

It would be naive to say that it is impossible to find information on recognition networks and national ENIC/NARIC centres. Typing "academic recognition" into the Google™ search engine reveals more than 10 pages of useful links with the homepage of ENIC/NARIC Networks at the top of the first page. But it seems that such information is traditionally considered "not interesting" by the academic community.

Recognition issues and solutions in the Bologna Process

A study carried out by an ENIC/NARIC working group sought to identify the recognition issues essential for the Bologna Process and the steps to be taken to resolve these issues [5]. Progress in the Bologna Process over the last couple of years has further clarified some of the issues, some achievements are visible and some new problems have been identified.

Recognition and the reform of degree structures

The ongoing reform of degree structures and the movement towards a two-tier structure across the whole of the European Higher Education Area have no doubt, had an impact on recognition.

The harmonisation of degree structures will benefit transparency and comparability. But the introduction of a flexible bachelor/master structure will also lead to more diversity [14]. In January 2001 the Bologna seminar on bachelor's degrees established a common framework for the workload and level of bachelor's degrees. But it also concluded that "programmes leading to the [bachelor's] degree may, and indeed should have different orientations and various profiles in order to accommodate a diversity of individual, academic and labour market needs" [15].

As regards master's degrees, the *Trends II* report [16] (pp. 28-29) indicated that master's degrees in Europe had at least seven different purposes and that the introduction of two-tier structures in the non-university/professional stream of higher education was further increasing this diversity. The European University Association (EUA) report on master's degrees in Europe [17] confirmed such diversity during the master's phase. The Helsinki seminar on master's degrees in March 2003, among other conclusions, acknowledged the diversity at master's level and concluded that "diversification of contents and profile of degree programmes calls for a common framework of reference of European higher education qualifications in order to increase transparency" [18].

The above means that there might be huge differences between degrees bearing the same name, in terms of admission requirements, content, learning objectives and function, as well as in the rights they confer. Thus, harmonisation of degree structures will lead to a greater transparency, but not to "automatic recognition" [14]. The need for individual recognition will still be there: while, in an idealised case, the *level* of the foreign qualification could possibly be recognised more or less "automatically", the main accent in the credential evaluation will be on interpretation of the foreign qualification in the context of the host country's higher education system and/or labour market.

Quality assurance – a necessary precondition for recognition

The increased importance of quality assurance and the acceptance of the close link between the quality assurance and recognition of institutions and study programmes on the one hand and individual qualifications on the other hand have had a major importance in improving the recognition of qualifications across the European Higher Education Area. At the time of adoption of the Lisbon Recognition Convention in 1997 discussions were still ongoing in Europe as to *whether* quality assurance was needed as a general norm. Far from all countries party to the Convention had established quality assurance systems at that time. Thus, while the notion of the importance of quality and quality assurance in the recognition of qualifications appears several times in the Convention text, it was not yet possible to link recognition of individual qualifications to quality assurance of the awarding institutions/programme as a necessary precondition.

Politically, the close link between quality assurance and recognition was underlined in the ministers' Prague Communiqué (May 2001) [19]. Since spring 2002 common issues of recognition and quality assurance have been analysed by a joint working group of the ENIC and NARIC recognition networks and ENQA.[18]

---

18. ENQA: European Assocaition for Quality Assurance: http://www.enqa.net

The ENIC and NARIC Networks fully support the principle that the recognition of qualifications should be made contingent on the provider of education having been subjected to transparent quality assessment [20].

It is important to admit that, should the recognition of individual qualifications be made directly linked to quality assurance of the institutions/programmes in question, it must also be ensured that the education providers have adequate access to quality assessment, regardless of whether the providers are public or private, a part of the national higher education system or not, leading to a full qualification or not. The issue of gaining access to assessment is especially important, for example, to serious transnational education providers, "international" institutions that do not belong to any of the educational systems of the countries in which they operate. Here one should also consider the providers of "non-degree programmes" or modules for the needs of lifelong learners – that is, the learning that does not lead to a final higher education qualification, but is of a level and quality that allows learners to claim credits for higher education. In all these cases access to quality assurance is not a trivial matter at present. Another issue still awaiting solution is the issue of non-accredited/non-quality-assessed programmes provided (in many cases perfectly legally) by recognised higher education institutions. The above means that accredited/non-accredited does not necessarily correspond to good/bad [14]. There are too many students in Europe today who study in valuable but non-accredited programmes for them to be simply declared "outlaws" when it comes to recognition.

It should also be borne in mind that for the sake of recognition of individual qualifications abroad, it is necessary that the outcomes of quality assessments are made public, whenever possible, in a widely spoken European language so that international credential evaluators can easily access and use them.

There is also some evidence that information on quality assurance outcomes is provided in a structured way, especially for the needs of recognition for the labour market: "information on quality from other countries needs to be properly channelled or 'translated' " [14].

Knowledge about the standard of institutions and the programmes they offer is of the utmost importance for credential evaluation. Yet to avoid a common misunderstanding, one must bear in mind that, while quality assurance is a *necessary* precondition for recognition of individual qualification, it is *not enough* in itself [14]. Knowledge of quality (and accreditation) alone is not an adequate basis for evaluating a qualification. To position it correctly in the education system or labour market of the receiving country, one needs a thorough knowledge of the system that conferred the qualification [21]. As shown in the previous chapter, this will not essentially change with the introduction of the two-cycle system throughout Europe.

Progress in less traditional recognition cases: transnational education, joint degrees, lifelong learning

Transnational education

The growing phenomenon of transnational education globally and in Europe has raised a number of issues, among them recognition of the qualifications earned transnationally. To address recognition issues of transnational education, the ENIC and NARIC Networks organised a working party that came up with an analysis of this phenomenon. Recognition problems of transnational education qualifications are often caused by the fact that transnational education programmes, as "foreign" ones, are not quality-checked by the receiving country, but, as programmes provided abroad, they are also removed from the quality assurance system of the sending country. The main concerns reported by the receiving countries are the following: doubts about the proficiency of the staff involved in the provision of transnational education, evidence that sometimes the transnational programmes are very different from those provided in the awarding institution itself, and evidence that transnational education qualifications are sometimes "easy" – that is, either the study time is shorter or the admission/graduation requirements are lower [22]. A detailed study on transnational education as a whole was funded by the EU and administered by the EUA [23].

All findings confirmed that the main recognition problems of transnational education qualifications were rooted in lack of transparency and lack of proper quality assurance, especially that of the actual education provision in the receiving country, often obscured by the lack of clarity surrounding the division of responsibilities between the mother institution, the actual providers abroad and agents acting between both the above parties and the officials of the receiving country. The UNESCO/Council of Europe working party drew up a Code of Good Practice for the Provision of Transnational Education [11], which was adopted in June 2001.

The code states that the awarding institution is responsible for the whole provision of transnational education, including the quality of programme delivery at the providing institution, the requirements for admission and graduation as well as the actions of the agents involved and the information they give to the students or the receiving country's officials.

The provision of transnational education should comply with the national legislation in both receiving and sending countries. Academic quality and standards of transnational education programmes as well as requirements regarding staff proficiency should be at least comparable to those of the awarding institution as well as to those of the receiving country. The admission of students, the teaching/learning activities, the examination and assessment requirements and the academic workload for transnational study programmes should be equivalent to those for the same or comparable programmes delivered by the awarding institution. Special attention is paid to the transparency of the delivery of transnational education and the provision of full and reliable information at the request of the receiving country's authorities. The qualifications issued through transnational programmes, complying with the provisions of the code, should be assessed in accordance with the stipulations of the Lisbon Recognition Convention.

Thus, the international legislation allowing the recognition of transnational higher education qualifications from bona fide providers is in place. However, it is just part of the solution of the issue. Several problems remain. The transnational education providers, as well as those who receive transnational education qualifications for assessment (especially the credential evaluators based in higher education institutions), are not always aware of the existence of the code. Also, reluctance is observed both on the part of transnational education providers to submit information about the education they provide[19] and on the part of national authorities, which sometimes still attempt – directly or indirectly – to outlaw the transnational education phenomenon as such, or simply avoid a dialogue with transnational education providers active in their countries. While some transnational education providers deliberately stay in the "grey zone" and are not willing to undergo quality assurance by the receiving country, it is not certain that a transnational education provider which seeks to be legally established in the receiving country will easily obtain access to quality assurance.

---

19. A UNESCO working party in 2003-2004 attempted to establish a database on transnational education, but it faced major difficulties in obtaining information from transnational education providers even when addressing individual transnational education providers directly (the working party will report on its results at the ENIC/NARIC Joint meeting in Strasbourg, June 2004).

A joint activity of OECD and UNESCO started in spring 2004 in order to establish guidelines for quality provision in cross-border higher education that will allow further progress on the issue. A final drafting meeting took place in Paris in January 2005. While the final version of the OECD-UNESCO Guidelines is not available at the time of writing, it can be seen from the draft document [24] that all parties – national governments, quality assurance agencies, competent recognition authorities, as well as the cross-border education providers themselves, should fulfil certain tasks in order to improve the recognition of qualifications earned transnationally. The national governments are encouraged to ensure that cross-border education providers have access to the quality assurance in place in their countries, and operate according to the national rules and regulations. The national quality assurance agencies are encouraged to apply the principles reflected in current international documents on cross-border higher education such as the UNESCO/Council of Europe Code of Good Practice in the Provision of Transnational Education, and to provide clear information on the criteria for the assessment of qualifications, including qualifications resulting from cross-border provision.

At the same time, the higher education institutions involved in cross-border provision should provide complete descriptions of programmes and qualifications, setting out details of the knowledge, understanding and skills that a successful student should acquire.

Joint degrees

Establishing programmes leading to joint degrees is seen as a useful tool towards achieving the European Higher Education Area [19]. A Bologna Process seminar on joint degrees was held in Stockholm in May 2002. The seminar indicated some problems pointing to the need to amend national legislation in order to make joint degrees a reality [25]. As demonstrated by the EUA's joint degrees survey published in September 2002 [26], work on joint degree programmes has stimulated implementation of practically all the Bologna Declaration lines of action, starting with establishing joint quality assurance, improving recognition, improving employability of graduates across Europe, and increasing mobility of students and teachers, and so on.

The main obstacles for establishing joint degrees are lack of appropriate provisions in the national legislation, and the fact that the current international legal framework for recognition applies only to national qualifications, while joint degrees in the strict legal sense do not belong to national higher education system, at least not to a single one. As regards amending national legislations, in their Berlin Communiqué of

19 September 2003 the European ministers agreed to take action at national level to remove legal obstacles to the establishment and recognition of joint degrees [5]. The EUA conference on joint degrees in Cluj, Romania, in October 2003 led to a set of practical recommendations with regard to co-operation among partners in establishing joint degrees [27].

A major development under the EU's Socrates programme is the Erasmus Mundus programme[20], which is designed to assist in establishing joint degrees and also contains some specific provisions for improving recognition of joint degrees, first of all between the partner institutions and countries.[21]

In order to improve the international recognition of joint degrees, the ENIC and NARIC Networks drafted a recommendation on the recognition of joint degrees, which was adopted by the Lisbon Recognition Convention Intergovernmental Committee in June 2004 [12]. The recommendation sets out to extend the main principles of the Convention to joint degrees, stipulating that the holder of a joint degree has a right to a fair assessment of his or her joint degree, and establishing that a joint degree is to be recognised unless substantial differences can be clearly demonstrated between the joint degree in question and the awarding host country's qualification. The recommendation also sets down requirements that should be fulfilled as a precondition for applying the Lisbon Convention principles to a joint degree: each part of the joint curriculum has to be quality-assessed or to be a part of a recognised national qualification; if the joint degree in question is awarded in the name of a larger consortium, care should be taken that each consortium partner is a trustworthy institution; the Diploma Supplement and ECTS should be used as transparency tools; and the joint character of the award should be clearly indicated and described.

Lifelong learning

Lifelong learning (LLL) has been addressed in all the Bologna Process political documents, starting with the Bologna Declaration itself. Indeed, lifelong learning activities as such are very widespread and growing; many higher education institutions provide courses for lifelong learners. However, the full integration of lifelong learning into regular higher education activities with a view to defining alternative study paths for lifelong learners that would allow them to attain regular higher education qualifications is an issue yet to be resolved. A Bologna seminar on recog-

---

20. Part of the Socrates programme of activities.
21. See: http://europa.eu.int/comm/education/programmes/mundus/index_en.html

nition and credit systems in the context of lifelong learning [28], held in Prague in June 2003, addressed the issues of integrating LLL into higher education activities and defining learning paths. The seminar recommendations also encourage higher education institutions to adopt internal policies to promote the recognition of prior formal, non-formal and informal learning for access and study exemption; and to reconsider skills content in courses and the nature of their study programmes, while the national authorities should ensure the right to fair recognition of qualifications acquired in different learning environments.

In the terms of the Lisbon Recognition Convention, lifelong learning paths would then be a part of the higher education systems of the States Parties, which also means that the qualifications thus earned would be considered for recognition on a par with the same qualifications earned through more traditional higher education learning paths. A second issue is how these learning paths could then be adequately described through transparency instruments such as the Diploma Supplement, ECTS and possibly a lifelong learning portfolio [29].

The seminar in Prague concluded that on the international scale it could be feasible to seek to develop international good practice to promote the recognition of qualifications earned through lifelong learning paths, using the provisions and principles of the Lisbon Recognition Convention; if feasible, to develop international instruments to facilitate such recognition; and to bring together existing experience with national qualifications frameworks with a view to facilitating the development of further national frameworks as well as a qualifications framework for the European Higher Education Area that would encompass lifelong learning paths [28].

A major development in the integration of LLL into regular higher education activities should be expected together with the establishing of national qualifications frameworks (see below), which, according to the request by the ministers in their Berlin Communiqué, should seek to describe the qualifications in terms of their level, workload, learning outcomes and profile, and "encompass the wide range of flexible learning paths, opportunities and techniques and to make appropriate use of the ECTS credits" [6].

Focusing on learning outcomes – high expectations from qualifications frameworks

To properly position a foreign qualification in the context of another country's higher education or employment system, the focus of credential

38

evaluation should be shifted from input characteristics, which may vary in different countries and higher education institutions, towards learning outcomes and competencies acquired. The need to shift to assessing learning outcomes has been already acknowledged in the Recommendation on Criteria and Procedures for the Assessment of Foreign Qualifications:

> "Competent recognition authorities and other assessment agencies should be encouraged to focus on the learning outcomes and competencies, as well as the quality of the delivery of an educational programme and to consider its duration as merely one indication of the level of achievement reached at the end of the programme" [10] (paragraph 40).

Assessing learning outcomes becomes even more important in less traditional cases – evaluation of transnational education qualifications, joint degrees, and (parts of) studies pursued in the context of lifelong learning. Moreover, when assessing qualifications for the needs of employers, "what the holder of the qualification can do" is highly important, while the information on the number of study hours in each course or which textbooks have been covered may appear of very limited importance.

However, "assessing learning outcomes" is easier said than done.

Thus, while the main accent on learning outcomes rather than duration of studies and other input characteristics was fully acknowledged in the Lisbon Recognition Convention and especially in its subsidiary texts, until recently there have been very few attempts in Europe to start describing qualifications in terms of learning outcomes. For this reason, credential evaluators have so far only been able to attempt to estimate the learning outcomes on the basis of the contents and duration of the programme.

In the recent past, two different initiatives have started which attempt to link the Bologna cycles or developments along subject lines with learning outcomes at "European" level.[22] The Joint Quality Initiative (JQI) started as an attempt to produce descriptors for bachelor's and master's levels [30], linking them with very generally formulated learning outcomes. During 2004 the JQI also developed descriptors (labelled as

---

22. The word "European" is loaded with different meanings. In the higher education sense it ranges from geographical Europe and countries belonging to the European Cultural Convention to meaning EU member states, countries participating in the Bologna Process, and is sometimes used to label activities conducted jointly by several counties located in Europe. We have tried to avoid the use of "European" in this text. It seemed impossible to avoid the use of "European" here because the use of "international" might have been understood to mean developments on a broader "world" scale.

Dublin descriptors) for short programmes of higher education as well as for the third (doctoral) Bologna cycle. From the recognition point of view the Dublin descriptors can only be used for very general guidance, while they are too general for use in the assessment of individual qualifications. Yet the Dublin descriptors have been found to be useful as cycle descriptors for the European overarching qualifications framework [31].

Another recent and highly valuable initiative, the Tuning project [32], seeks to establish learning outcomes along subject lines. In particular, prior to defining subject-specific competencies, several groups of generic competencies have been identified and their relative importance for various stakeholders analysed.

The most important initiative with a view to the overall improvement of recognition across the European Higher Education Area, however, is the emergence of qualifications frameworks – both the national ones and the overarching European framework. A national qualifications framework is nothing more than a precise description of the structure of the national qualifications system, indicating the workload, level and learning outcomes of each qualification and the sequence in which the qualifications follow each other [33]. Although one could argue that each country has some kind of national qualifications framework already, the first systematic attempts to describe qualifications in terms of level, workload, profile and learning outcomes are just emerging. The discussions at the Copenhagen seminar on qualifications frameworks on 27 and 28 March 2003 demonstrated [34] that the introduction of qualifications frameworks should help recognition of qualifications across the European Higher Education Area because the "new-type" description of qualifications through level, workload, learning outcomes and profile provides exactly the information about qualifications that was previously missing, making it possible to find out how a foreign qualification can be used in the context of the host country. Acknowledging the usefulness of qualifications frameworks for the goals of the Bologna Process the ministers, in their Berlin Communiqué of 2003:

> "encourage the member States to elaborate a framework of comparable and compatible qualifications for their higher education systems, which should seek to describe qualifications in terms of workload, level, learning outcomes, competences and profile. They also undertake to elaborate an overarching framework of qualifications for the European Higher Education Area." [6]

Accordingly, a Bologna working group on qualifications frameworks was established and it came up with a report [31] which describes the main features of the European overarching qualifications framework as well as an outline for the national qualifications frameworks. The overarching framework for qualifications of the EHEA is deliberately made very general, as it should not replace the national frameworks but rather articulate them and help in interpreting qualifications between different national frameworks. The levels in the overarching framework are those at the end of each of the three Bologna cycles and the Dublin descriptors are used to describe each cycle and also to describe the short programme of higher education within the first cycle. The new-style national qualifications frameworks plus the European overarching framework are expected to stimulate fair recognition in various ways.

Articulating the national frameworks against the overarching European framework is helpful for comparing the level of national qualifications from different higher education systems.

As the national frameworks will be based upon learning outcomes, it will be much easier to focus credential evaluation of those particular learning outcomes which are relevant to the purpose for which recognition is sought rather than comparing more formal aspects of the qualification. Knowledge of learning outcomes should also make it easier to grant partial recognition in those cases where full recognition is impossible. Expressing the aims of study programmes and each of their parts in terms of learning outcomes should also stimulate the assignment of credits for achievements from prior (experiential) learning.

Thus, the expectations for the impact of qualifications frameworks on recognition are high. And therefore the risks should also not be left unnoticed. The risks are the following. First of all, many of the countries involved in the Bologna Process have no experience in formulating learning outcomes. To formulate learning outcomes correctly staff will need appropriate training [35]. Generally, if national qualifications frameworks are devised superficially or without the proper involvement of all the stakeholders, they may create more misunderstandings than benefits. Finally, for recognition purposes it is extremely important that the elaboration of the national qualifications frameworks does not end after formulation of the common learning outcomes for generic qualifications. To benefit recognition of individual qualifications, it is important that subject-specific learning outcomes are also described for qualifications in different fields.

Are the transparency tools suitable for taking in information on learning outcomes and qualifications frameworks?

The two main existing transparency tools – ECTS and the Diploma Supplement – are highly useful and facilitate recognition. At the current stage of developments in the Bologna Process one may rightly ask whether the Diploma Supplement and ECTS are ready for the new situation: can they accommodate information on qualifications in terms of learning outcomes and can they consider qualifications frameworks?

ECTS, which has been widely used for credit transfer in student exchanges, was recently developed from a credit transfer to a credit transfer and accumulation system. Since autumn 2004 ECTS has been called "European Credit Transfer and Accumulation System". Furthermore, the recent development of ECTS links credits with learning outcomes. To quote the "ECTS Key features" document in its version updated on 27 July 2004:

> "The European Credit Transfer and Accumulation System is a student-centred system based on the *student workload* required to achieve the objectives of a programme ... objectives are preferably specified in terms of the *learning outcomes* and competences to be acquired." [36]

The way in which the credits should be allocated in the "upgraded" ECTS system clearly links credits with learning outcomes:

> "Credits are allocated to all educational components of a study programme (such as modules, courses, placements, dissertation work, and so on) and reflect the quantity of work each component requires to achieve its specific objectives or learning outcomes in relation to the total quantity of work necessary to complete a full year of study successfully." [36]

The Diploma Supplement, among other useful information for the qualification, contains an indication of the purposes for which the qualification may be used in the holder's further studies or employment in the country where the qualification has been issued. This information is highly useful for credential evaluators abroad, yet it gives a very general indication of learning outcomes. However, the Diploma Supplement in its existing format is already able to accommodate the information on both the national qualifications frameworks and the learning outcomes associated with the qualification to which the Diploma Supplement has been issued.

As can be seen from the Explanatory notes [37] for those producing Diploma Supplements[23] the guidance for filling in the Diploma Supplement point 4.2 (Programme requirements) includes:

---

23. The Diploma Supplement working group that devised the Diploma Supplement format also created a set of guidance documents to use when creating diploma supplements. Although publicised in 1998 together with the now widely used Diploma Supplement, these documents unfortunately are less well known.

"provide details of the learning outcomes, skills, competencies and stated aims and objectives associated with the qualification."

The description of the national qualifications framework should be included in the Diploma Supplement point 8 (Information on the national higher education system):

> "give information on the ... types of institution and the qualifications structure. This description should provide a context for the qualification and refer to it." [37]

Thus, although the Diploma Supplement has not been used for these purposes in the past, it is suitable for accommodating information about learning outcomes and competencies linked to the qualification in question, as well as about the national qualifications framework. The other main transparency tool, ECTS, has after its recent adaptation become a credit system for accumulation too and is able to accommodate the information on learning outcomes linked to the particular credits. In this way, these transparency tools have become even more useful for the purposes of recognition of individual qualifications.

Recognition between the EHEA and other parts of the world

One of the major goals of establishing the European Higher Education Area is to improve the attractiveness and raise the overall competitiveness of European higher education in the world. This means that, while reforming degree structures and ensuring the recognition of qualifications among countries belonging to the European Higher Education Area, care should also be taken to promote recognition of European qualifications in the outside world. When deciding upon a major reform – the introduction of a two-tier degree system across Europe – the logical assumption was that this should improve understanding and, hence, recognition of European degrees outside. Indeed, when comparing degree systems across the world, the most common is the system with two tiers of degrees, usually called bachelor's and master's degrees, at least in the English translation. As preliminary discussions with experts from other parts of the world show, in quite a large number of systems, especially in Asia and Africa, it will ease understanding and recognition of a foreign degree if the degree can be classified as a "bachelor's" or "master's".

However, the issue seems easy only at first sight. When considering how Bologna reforms could influence the perception of European degrees outside Europe, a number of issues should be taken into account.

First of all, although no official Bologna Process document stipulates such a pattern, in a number of European countries the Bologna reforms are being implemented as a transition to a "3+2" system, meaning a first-cycle (bachelor's) degree worth 180 ECTS credits (three years of studies) and a second-cycle (master's) degree worth 120 ECTS credits (two years of studies). At the same time, in other parts of the world the bachelor's degree is quite often awarded after a workload that takes four years of full-time studies, and it can be followed by a master's degree requiring one, one and a half or even two years of studies.

The recognition of the European three-year bachelor's degrees outside Europe is therefore an issue to be urgently discussed, especially with North American higher education systems. There is speculation on both sides: while North Americans may point to shorter study programmes in Europe, Europeans usually point to differences in secondary education systems and the inclusion of general subjects in the first years of bachelor's studies.

Another group of questions is related to the perception of bachelor's and master's degrees. Some higher education systems in the world treat the master's degree as a genuine postgraduate degree (which at the same time means that the bachelor's degree is treated without any doubt as a meaningful level of higher education and the holder of a bachelor's degree as "already" a graduate). As regards Europe, and particularly continental Europe, such a perception of bachelor's and master's degrees has yet to be formed. It seems that the bachelor's degree in a number of countries is rather seen as a first stage of studies and that most holders of bachelor's degrees are actually expected to continue their studies to get "the real thing".

The above issues may have their impact on recognition (and especially recognition of first degrees) between Europe and the other parts of the world, especially North America.

The exact answers to all the above questions can only be found when the actual learning outcomes can be compared between both sides. However, the development of learning outcomes-based qualifications frameworks in many of the EHEA countries is just at its initial stage. In some other parts of the world the discussion of expressing qualifications using learning outcomes has not even started. Yet the recognition issues are there and cannot wait while the entire world starts using learning outcomes. The debate concerning recognition of Bologna degrees, first of all within the North American higher education systems, has to be started immediately, and an intensive information campaign regarding the new "Bologna degrees" and qualifications frameworks should be a part of it.

Conclusions

Improving recognition of qualifications earned in one of the Bologna Process countries across all other Bologna Process countries is a necessary precondition for successfully establishing the European Higher Education Area. The international legal framework for recognition within the European Higher Education Area is established and developing. The international "recognition community" is following new developments and drawing up new international legal instruments to cover the emerging needs.

For the recognition of qualifications in the European Higher Education Area it is essential that, first of all, the core legal document for recognition – the Lisbon Recognition Convention – is ratified in all the Bologna countries, and this process is progressing significantly. However, the further national and institutional implementation of the legal framework for recognition seems to be a much weaker point. As in several other Bologna Process aspects, we are approaching the limits of what can be done at European or international level. Further success requires the involvement of national authorities, and, what is much more difficult to achieve, all levels of higher education staff. A major effort and intensive information campaigns should take place in all Bologna countries with a view to:

- actually embedding the principles of the Convention into both national legislation and institutional policies,

- substantially raising institutional awareness at all levels regarding recognition issues and the international legal framework,

- creating and implementing institutional recognition practices,

- last but not least, creating a positive attitude towards foreign qualifications and a willingness to find how they can be used in the host countries.

Introduction of the two-tier degree structure across Europe will benefit transparency and comparability, but it will also create a greater diversity, which means that it will not lead to automatic recognition between different parts of the European Higher Education area.

Linking recognition of individual qualifications to the information on quality is a widely accepted principle, but it is also an indication that such information should be available and should be in a form useful for the assessment of individual qualifications. However, knowledge of quality (and accreditation) alone is not an adequate basis for evaluating a qualification; a thorough knowledge of the system that conferred the qualification is necessary to position it correctly in the education system or labour market of the receiving country.

As regards recognition of lifelong learning, the main accent should be put on establishing learning paths that make it possible to attain higher education qualifications in an alternative way. Once lifelong learning studies have resulted in a regular form of national higher education, international recognition is not the most complex issue.

The importance of assessing learning outcomes and not input parameters in the recognition of qualifications has been stressed already in the framework of the Lisbon Convention. The Bologna Process and the emergence of various types of non-traditional qualifications strengthens this need. At the same time, while the transparency of qualifications in general is growing, qualifications in current practice are not described in terms of learning outcomes. The commitment to establish national qualifications frameworks describing qualifications in terms of level, workload, learning outcomes and profile, with an overarching framework for the European Higher Education Area as a whole, is an opportunity for substantial improvements in understanding between European higher education systems and, as a consequence, recognition of qualifications.

The two main transparency tools of qualifications – the Diploma Supplement and ECTS are suitable for accommodating information relating to qualifications frameworks and expressing qualifications in terms of learning outcomes, and therefore remain useful tools for these new tasks as well.

One of the most important conclusions of this chapter is also that the understanding and recognition of the new European degrees in other parts of the world will not come automatically. An information campaign and a debate with other parts of the world should be started as soon as possible.

References

1. Convention on the Recognition of Qualifications concerning Higher Education in the European Region. European Treaty Series No. 165, Council of Europe/ UNESCO joint convention, 1997, 23 p. // Internet: http://www.cepes.ro/information_services/sources/on_line/lisbon.htm

2. Sorbonne Joint Declaration on harmonisation of the architecture of the European higher education system by the four ministers in charge for France, Germany, Italy and the United Kingdom, 1998, 3 p. // Internet: http://www.bologna-berlin2003.de/pdf/Sorbonne_declaration.pdf

3. The European Higher Education Area. Joint Declaration of the European Ministers of Education convened in Bologna on 19 June 1999 // Internet http://www.bologna-bergen2005.no

4. Seminar "Recognition issues in the Bologna Process", Lisbon, 11-12 April 2002. Final report by Lewis Purser. // Internet: http://www.aic.lv/ace/publicat/2003/05_annex_II.rtf

5. Realising the European Higher Education Area – Communiqué of the Conference of Ministers responsible for Higher Education in Berlin on 19 September 2003. Internet: http://www.bologna-berlin2003.de/pdf/Communique1.pdf

6. Recognition issues in the Bologna Process. Final report of the ENIC/NARIC Working Party on Recognition Issues in the Bologna Process, 2001. // Internet http://www.aic.lv/ace/ace_disk/Bologna/Reports/research/Rec_bol.rtf

7. Bergan, Sjur, Jindra Divis and Andrejs Rauhvargers. "Bridges over troubled waters: Bologna and recognition of qualifications", *Journal of Studies in International Education*, Vol. 4., No. 2, pp. 61-87.

8. Council of Europe/UNESCO Recommendation on International Access Qualifications, adopted 1999, // Internet http://www.cepes.ro/hed/recogn/groups/recomm.htm

9. Reichert, Sybille and Christian Tauch. *Trends 2003*: Progress towards the European Higher Education Area, European Association, Geneva/Brussels, 2003, 131 p.

10. Council of Europe/UNESCO Recommendation on Criteria and Procedures for the Assessment of Foreign Qualifications, adopted June 2001 // Internet http://www.cepes.ro/hed/recogn/groups/criteria.htm

11. Council of Europe/UNESCO Code of Good Practice for the Provision of Transnational Education, adopted on 6 June 2001. // Internet http://www.cepes.ro/hed/recogn/groups/transnat/code.htm

12. Council of Europe/UNESCO Recommendation for the Recognition of Joint Degrees, submitted for adoption in June 2004. // Internet http://www.aic.lv/ace/ace_disk/Recognition/leg_aca/JD_recom.rtf

13. Bergan, Sjur. "Implementation of Lisbon Convention and Contributions to the Bologna Process". In: *Recognition issues in the Bologna Process*. Council of Europe Publishing 2003, pp. 69-84.

14. Divis, Jindra. Bologna and qualifications: quality, recognition, credit and accreditation in international perspective. Paper presented at the 10th Joint Meeting of the ENIC/NARIC Networks, Vaduz, Liechtenstein, 2003, 14 p.

15. Bologna Process seminar on bachelor-level degrees – conclusions and recommendations, Helsinki, Finland, 16-17 February 2001, http://www.aic.lv/ace/ace_disk/Bologna/Bol_semin/Helsinki/hel_bac.pdf

16. Haug, Guy and Christian Tauch, Christian. *Trends in learning structures in higher education (II)*. Report for the Salamanca Academic Convention and Prague Ministerial Conference. Published by National Board of Education of Finland, Helsinki, 2001, 90 p. // Internet: http://www.bologna-berlin2003.de/pdf/trend_II.pdf

17. Tauch, Christian. "Master degrees in the European Higher Education Area", in Tauch, C. and A. Rauhvargers. *Survey on master degrees and joint degrees in Europe*, EUA, Brussels, 2002, pp. 7-25.

18. Conclusions and recommendations of the Bologna Conference on master-level degrees, Helsinki, 14-15 March 2003, 5.p. // Internet: http://www.bologna-berlin2003.de/pdf/Results.pdf

19. Towards the European Higher Education Area. Communiqué of the meeting of European Ministers in charge of Higher Education in Prague on 19 May 2001. // Internet: http://www.cepes.ro/information_services/sources/on_line/prague.htm

20. Statement by the ENIC and NARIC Networks on the European Higher Education Area (Vaduz statement) adopted at the joint ENIC/NARIC meeting, 18-20 May 2003. // Internet: http://www.enic-naric.net/documents/VaduzStatement2003.pdf

21. Rauhvargers, Andrejs. "Recognition: from acknowledgement of foreign diplomas to an essential part of the Bologna Process", in

Recognition issues in the Bologna Process. Council of Europe Publishing, 2003, pp 55-67.

22. Rauhvargers, Andrejs. "Recognition in the European region: response to recent challenges from inside and outside", in *Globalization and the market in Higher Education*, UNESCO Publishing, 2002, pp. 73-82.

23. Adam, Stephen. Transnational education project report and recommendations, March 2001, 53 p. // Internet: http://gerda.univie.ac.at/redsys/doc_bolognalab// transnational_education_project_Adam.pdf

24. Draft Guidelines for quality provision in cross-border higher education, jointly elaborated between the OECD and UNESCO, Paris, 7 January 2005. Internet: http://www.oecd.org/dataoecd/33/8/34258720.pdf

25. Conclusions and recommendations of the Seminar on Joint Degrees within the framework of the Bologna Process, Stockholm, May 31, 2002 3p. // Internet: http://www.bologna-berlin2003.de/pdf/Stockholm_results.pdf

26. Rauhvargers, Andrejs. "Joint degree study", in C. Tauch and A. Rauhvargers. *Survey on master degrees and joint degrees in Europe*, EUA, Brussels, 2002. pp. 27-43.

27. EUA Conference on Joint Degrees, "Institutions working together at European Level", Cluj, Romania, 24-25 October 2003. // Internet: http://www.eua.be/eua/en/eua_conferences_past_chuj.htm

28. Recommendations of the Bologna seminar on recognition and credit systems in the context of lifelong learning, Prague, 5-7 June 2003. // Internet: http://www.bologna-berlin2003.de/pdf/recommendations.pdf

29. Bergan, Sjur. Final report of the Bologna Process seminar on credit systems and recognition in the context of lifelong learning, Prague, 5-7 June 2003. // Internet: http://www.bologna-berlin2003.de/pdf/report_SjurBergan.pdf

30 Towards shared descriptors of bachelors and masters, Joint Quality Initiative working group, 2002, 4 p. // Internet: http://www.jointquality.org/

31 A Framework for Qualifications of the European Higher Education Area. Report of the Bologna Working Group on Qualifications Frameworks, Copenhagen 2005, 200 p.

32. *Tuning Educational structures in Europe. Final report Phase 1*, Bilbao, 2003, 316 p. // Internet: http://tuning.unideusto.org/tuningeu/

33. Adam, Stephen. Background report for the Bologna seminar on qualification structures in higher education in Europe, 27-28 March 2003, Copenhagen, Denmark, 63 p. // Internet: http://www.vtu.dk/fsk/div/bologna/BasicReportforSeminar.pdf

34. Bergan, Sjur. Final report of the Bologna seminar on qualification structures in higher education in Europe 27-28 March 2003, Copenhagen, Denmark, 19 p. // Internet: http://www.vtu.dk/fsk/div/bologna/ Koebenhavn_Bologna_Reprot_final.pdf

35. Bologna conference on qualifications frameworks, Copenhagen, 13-14 January 2005. Report by the general rapporteur Sjur Bergan, 26 p. // Internet:http://www.bologna-bergen2005.no/EN/Bol_sem/ Seminars/050113-14Copenhagen/050113-14_General_report.pdf

36. European Credit Transfer and Accumulation System (ECTS). Key features. // Internet: http://europa.eu.int/comm/education/ programmes/socrates/ects/ectskey_en.pdf

37. Guidance documents to those producing Diploma Supplements: II (Explanatory notes). // Internet: http://www.aic.lv/ace/ace_disk/Dipl_Sup/

The impact of emerging qualifications frameworks on recognition

Stephen Adam

The Bologna Process is now gathering pace and a number of initiatives associated with it are already transforming higher education in the Europe region. This process is about to be augmented with some further innovations that will have profound effects on recognition. The developments in question are the creation of national qualifications frameworks and the overarching framework for qualifications of the European Higher Education Area (EHEA). The Berlin Communiqué included the following:

> "Ministers underline the importance of consolidating the progress made, and of improving understanding and acceptance of the new qualifications through reinforcing dialogue within institutions and between institutions and employers.
>
> Ministers encourage the member States to elaborate a framework of comparable and compatible qualifications for their higher education systems, which should seek to describe qualifications in terms of workload, level, learning outcomes, competences and profile. They also undertake to elaborate an overarching framework of qualifications for the European Higher Education Area.
>
> Within such frameworks, degrees should have different defined outcomes. First and second cycle degrees should have different orientations and various profiles in order to accommodate a diversity of individual, academic and labour market needs. First cycle degrees should give access, in the sense of the Lisbon Recognition Convention, to second cycle programmes. Second cycle degrees should give access to doctoral studies."

These simple statements place an emphasis on "qualifications", "qualifications frameworks" and an "overarching framework of qualifications" for the European Higher Education Area. In addition they highlight "workload", "level", "learning outcomes" and "profile". Collectively, the introduction of these new elements will have a profound impact on recognition, recognition tools, recognition processes and the transparency of national higher education systems.

It is important to explore the nature of this impact but this is not without some difficulties. Any attempt to predict the future must be treated with some caution. In particular, it is not possible to make definitive statements about the impact of the results of the Copenhagen Seminar of 13 and 14 January 2005 on the Framework for Qualifications and the European Higher Education Area. However, it is likely that the Bergen Communiqué, which emerges in May 2005, will strongly endorse the qualifications frameworks approach. Furthermore, many stakeholders have already reacted positively to the proposals made in the report on this topic produced by a Bologna Follow-up Group (BFUG) working party.[24]

The working group report explores, *inter alia*: good practice in the development of "new-style" national qualifications frameworks; the relationship between national qualifications frameworks and the overarching European framework for qualifications; and the features, impact and potential "added value" of such structures. "New-style" output-focused national frameworks that employ "workload, level, learning outcomes, competencies and profile" plus credits are very different from traditional input-focused approaches used to place and explain qualifications. Furthermore, frameworks provide more explicit and precise information in their qualifications descriptors and in their links to other external reference points. It is these features that will impact most on the recognition field.

It is no coincidence that in the recognition area there is a matching trend towards emphasising the "fair recognition" of qualifications based on what a person knows and is able to do, rather than on the formal procedures that have led to qualifications. Furthermore, in an effort to promote more accurate judgments of qualifications, it is apparent that detailed comparisons of the formal aspects of individual qualifications (curriculum content, status of institution, recommended textbooks, duration/contact hours, access requirements, and so on) give a less accurate basis for evaluation. It is more helpful when qualifications are situated within national qualifications frameworks that are characterised by a clear description of learning outcomes, supplemented by a consideration of level, workload and profile. A strong advantage of qualifications frameworks is that they can, for the purposes of comparison, provide a more accurate basis and explanation of qualifications.

The adoption and encouragement of national qualifications frameworks by the ministers in Berlin in 2003 (which was a central piece of the Bergen Ministerial Conference in 2005) represents a radical move to

---

24. This report, "The framework of Qualifications for the European Higher Education Area", can be found at http://www.bologna-bergen2005.no/

ensure that an effective and practical European Higher Education Area is created. It certainly represents a challenge to all those involved in recognition. Improved recognition can be seen as one of the preconditions for establishing an effective European Higher Education Area.

National qualifications frameworks and the overarching framework for qualifications of the European higher education area

A comprehensive restructuring of the European landscape of higher education is under way and qualifications themselves are becoming the focus of more attention as their meaning and relevance are being considered. Part of this process is a pronounced tendency to create more explicit systems that map and explain the purpose and relationship between different qualifications.

"New-style" national frameworks of qualifications employ learning outcomes, levels, level indicators and qualification descriptors as explicit reference points. There are various forms of national qualifications frameworks: some include all levels and types of qualifications while some separate higher education qualifications from other types of qualifications. Modern national qualification structures invariably involve much more than a simple distinction between two cycles and commonly include a range of qualifications, intermediate awards and levels.

National frameworks of qualifications in higher education can achieve certain things. They can make explicit the purposes and aims of qualifications – by their clear description through the articulation of the learning outcomes, and by clarifying any rights to professional practice and recognition associated with them. They can delineate points of integration and overlap between different qualifications and qualification types, thereby positioning qualifications in relation to one another and showing routes (and barriers) for progression. They can provide a nationally agreed framework that guides and reflects the agreement of stakeholders. Finally they can provide a context for the design, review, articulation and development of existing and new qualifications. National frameworks of qualifications can also act as drivers of change and can help to: promote the attainment of qualifications; raise the awareness of citizens and employers in relation to qualifications; support learners and clarify all the educational opportunities available to them; facilitate curriculum change, and so on.

It is quite properly a matter of national autonomy and concern what exactly the framework is designed to achieve. It is up to national authorities to decide priorities, the number of levels in any national system and the content and purpose of their qualifications. Qualifications are owned by national systems. The overarching framework for the EHEA derives its distinctive purposes from the objectives expressed through the Bologna Process. The most directly relevant of these objectives are international transparency, recognition, and mobility.

The overarching framework for qualifications of the European Higher Education Area will in reality be a framework of frameworks – an articulation mechanism between national frameworks. The overarching European framework will have to have distinctive objectives over and above those of national frameworks. It assists in the identification of points of articulation between national frameworks and serves as a point of reference for those developing or reviewing national frameworks of qualification. It expresses how the qualifications systems of the various states are related to each other, especially where these national systems have themselves been incorporated into formal national frameworks. It offers a common set of cycles (a broad form of level), with descriptors for those cycles. Much of the detail expressed in national frameworks is neither necessary nor desirable in an overarching framework. The framework for qualifications of the EHEA will not replace national frameworks but augment them by providing a series of reference points whereby they can demonstrate their mutual compatibility.

The relationship between qualifications frameworks and current recognition tools and practices

International transparency is at the heart of the Bologna Declaration's call for a system of easily readable and comparable degrees. Many other devices, such as the 1997 Council of Europe/UNESCO Convention on the Recognition of Qualifications Concerning Higher Education in the European Region (Lisbon Recognition Convention), the Diploma Supplement, European Credit Transfer and Accumulation Systems (ECTS), the Council of Europe/UNESCO European Network of Information Centres for Recognition and Mobility (ENIC) and the European Union Network of National Academic Information Centres (NARIC) have a role to play in this objective. Yet without a simplifying architecture for mutual understanding, such as a qualifications framework, it will be difficult to ensure that qualifications can be easily read and compared across borders. Moreover, the relatively rapid success in the introduction of the two-cycle model through much of the European Higher Education Area has in some ways already served to underline that a comparable structure of awards is not in itself sufficient for genuine comparability and transparency. If qualifications are just labelled as

"Bachelor" or "Master" this provides no common approach to standards or type; indeed, it can mask fundamental differences and bring the whole approach into disrepute. This realisation was the basis of the call in the Berlin Communiqué for an overarching framework to link the national frameworks together in a coherent way.

International recognition of qualifications builds on transparency. A framework which provides a common understanding of the outcomes represented by a qualification rather than a mere assertion of comparability will greatly enhance the usefulness of qualifications across the European Higher Education Area. A variety of purposes are associated with the international recognition of qualifications including employment, access to further qualifications, prior exemption from parts of studies, access to continuing education, enhancing mobility, and so on. The development of a common overarching framework through the collaborative efforts of stakeholders across Europe will enhance the other actions being made to improve recognition for these purposes.

The international mobility of learners depends on the recognition of their prior learning and qualifications gained. Learners moving between qualifications or cycles require recognition in order to access more advanced programmes. Students moving within their studies (and their advisers) can benefit from the clarity that may be provided through the specification of the level and nature of the study programmes. Learners can have greater confidence that the outcomes of study abroad will fully contribute to the qualification sought in their home country. A framework will be of particular help in supporting the development and recognition of joint degrees from more than one country. Joint degrees are likely to become widespread in the medium term and thus highly significant for the development of European education.

It is clear that qualifications frameworks are being promoted in order to have a beneficial effect on transparency, recognition and mobility. They are going to have an impact on existing recognition tools and practices. If they do not, the very rationale for their existence is undermined. A useful way to identify their precise potential benefits is to explore them in terms of a number of key questions associated with their use:

1. How will or might "new-style" qualifications frameworks improve recognition?

They can improve recognition by providing a detailed context within which national qualifications exist. Qualifications expressed in terms of learning outcomes can be understood more readily as they show what the learner can do after gaining the award. This clarifies our understanding of other European qualifications and helps in any evaluation process. New style qualifications frameworks also have the benefit of clear external reference points such as levels, level descriptors, qualification descriptors, together with information on workload and profile. These output-focused tools help place the qualification in a clear national context that aids the internal quality assurance regime. The international use of common approaches (not common curricula) and methodologies to express our qualifications makes national education systems themselves more easily readable and comparable. This helps to build confidence and what have been called "zones of mutual trust". As a result "fair recognition" should be enhanced.

2. What sort of links exist between credential evaluation, qualifications frameworks and quality assurance and what is their significance?

A direct connection exists between credential evaluation, qualifications frameworks and quality assurance. The development and use of explicit criteria and processes that are open to external scrutiny are a natural corollary of output-focused qualifications frameworks. External reference points form a useful part of any system that is based on autonomous, yet accountable, higher education institutions. Effective and open quality assurance helps to develop a firm basis for mutual trust between different national systems. There is likely to be increasing international interest in the comparability between national systems, their qualifications and the process and results of their mechanisms to ensure quality. Good credential evaluation is predicated on effective quality assurance processes and instruments. Therefore, the ethos and approach to credential evaluation should reflect the good practice principles embodied in any national approach to qualification frameworks and quality assurance.

3. What sort of impact will qualifications frameworks have on the work of the ENIC/ NARIC Networks and on credential evaluators within institutions?

The ENIC and NARIC Networks exist to co-operate and improve academic recognition of diplomas and periods of study. They also seek to resolve intractable recognition problems that arise between states. In this they can be assisted by qualifications frameworks in their provision of authoritative advice and information concerning recognition. They will be able to more easily interpret the new systems that share similar methodological assumptions and are linked to the overarching framework of qualifications for the European Higher Education Area.

The main users of ENIC and NARIC are higher education institutions, students and their advisers, parents, teachers and prospective employers. The existence of qualifications frameworks should enhance the quality of their advice and allow the clear explanation of the basis of decisions. This is particularly important for the application of the Council of Europe-UNESCO Lisbon Recognition Convention (1997). This binds countries that have ratified the Convention to:

–   make recognition decisions on the basis of appropriate information on the qualifications for which recognition is sought (Article III.2);

–   put a duty on institutions to provide relevant information to holders of their qualifications (Article III.3);

–   demonstrate substantial differences in the case of refusal (Article VI);

–   provide a description of higher education programmes (Article VIII.2);

–   put the responsibility to demonstrate that an application does not fulfil the relevant requirements on the body making the assessment (Article III.2), and so on.

It is clear that this good-practice approach is often not followed by the countries that have ratified the Convention. The use of qualifications frameworks should make it much easier for institutions to comply with all the articles in the Convention.

Credential evaluators in higher education institutions should similarly benefit. In particular they are already receiving increasing numbers of Diploma Supplements. These supplements will be able to place qualifications in transparent national qualifications frameworks as well as the overarching European framework. Furthermore, this approach can help take some of the load off the ENIC and NARIC Networks and free their resources to deal with more specialist recognition issues.

In addition to the general situation described above, ENIC and NARIC and credential evaluators will benefit from the specific use of learning outcomes. Learning outcomes are a fundamental part of national qualifications frameworks and the tools associated with them (level and qualification descriptors). In effect, they are the basic building blocks of "new style" output-focused systems. Modules and units and whole qualifications are expressed in terms of learning outcomes that provide the micro-level transparency which facilitates precise and accurate recognition decisions.

4. What might be the impact of qualifications frameworks on the recognition of specific issues?

There are a number of other recognition questions and issues that arise with the development of the Bologna Process. It is useful to explore some of these to see how the advent of qualifications frameworks might impact on them.

Qualifications frameworks will probably have an effect on the end qualifications associated with the Bologna cycles. The development of national "levels" and European "cycle" descriptors should ensure that qualifications are in the appropriate place. Level descriptors guide the curriculum designer and the learner. Qualifications descriptors should also help the correct placing of qualifications within frameworks. The insertion of qualifications in frameworks has to be justified in terms of explicit references points and not on custom and practice. The case of intermediate qualifications may be problematic in that the three broad generic European higher education cycles descriptors (developed from the Dublin descriptors) will provide limited guidance. The introduction of a short-cycle descriptor, within or linked to the first cycle, may well help but it will be for the appropriate national authorities to place their intermediate awards within their own national frameworks, which can be as complex as they think fit.

A further complication that will inevitably arise is the treatment of qualifications from the non-Bologna world. The assessment of these should be guided by the good practice already developed in Europe and embodied in the Lisbon Recognition Convention. Furthermore, the existence of domestic and Bologna region qualifications frameworks will provide firm reference points against which such qualifications can be assessed. A linked concern is the approach taken towards transnational education qualifications. This topic cannot be adequately treated here. It is often regarded as such a problematic area that is best ignored. Transnational (borderless) education [25] is a growing phenomenon and the advent of new education providers poses significant challenges to traditional patterns of education and the authorities responsible for them. Many countries continue to display a schizophrenic and negative attitude towards imported education whilst heavily promoting the exportation of their own. Transnational education should never be regarded per se as an inherently negative or positive phenomenon – rather it is a "fact of life" that cannot be "un-invented" or abolished. It touches on many dimensions of the cur-

---

25. Including corporate, for-profit, not-for-profit, franchises and branch campuses.

rent European educational debate engendered by the Bologna declaration, including matters of recognition, transparency, accreditation, cultural and academic autonomy, convergence and divergence. The competition it represents can sharpen our domestic education provisions and consequently the quality of educational exports, which in turn, can promote our distinctive European cultures worldwide. It can also lead to a dumbing-down of qualifications as competitive forces can reduce standards to the lowest common denominator.

Inaction towards transnational education on behalf of European providers (exporters), students, regulators, receiving countries (importers), and international organisations would harm the development of the European Higher Education Area. Transnational education certainly raises a number of difficult questions, in particular, how should public authorities fairly treat these new forms of education? The creation of qualifications frameworks can help create an effective approach to transnational education. They provide clear reference points against which transnational education programmes can be measured and given recognition within national systems. The 2001 UNESCO/Council of Europe *Code of Good Practice for the Provision of Transnational Education* would be strengthened by the precision that qualifications frameworks bring to national qualifications, which transnational providers would be required to emulate. They can help establish standards and aid the effectiveness of domestic quality assurance systems; thus rogue educational providers can be identified and the public warned.

Finally, qualifications frameworks can impact on the recognition of qualifications earned through lifelong learning. The impact depends on the policy and structures adopted by individual countries. Some countries are developing integrated qualifications framework that encompass all learning from the cradle to the grave (for example, the Scottish Credit and Qualifications Framework – SCQF). Within such systems the recognition of lifelong learning presents fewer problems. In the area of higher education many nations are developing approaches that recognise formal, non-formal and informal learning. Processes for the Accreditation of Prior Experiential Learning (APEL) are used to recognise learning wherever it took place and give access or exemption to prospective students on this basis. Qualifications frameworks that employ output-focused tools, particularly learning outcomes, facilitate the recognition of such examples of lifelong learning. The European Commission in November 2004 established an expert group to assist them in the rapid creation of a European Union blueprint – a qualifications framework that would encompass lifelong learning. This will link higher education and Vocational Education and Training (VET). Such a development has obvious implications for EU states and directly links qualifications frameworks and lifelong learning.

The potential benefits to recognition from qualifications frameworks

It can be seen from the above analysis that there are a number of potential benefits that emerging qualifications frameworks should bring to the recognition area. These can be summarised as follows. Qualifications frameworks:

- improve the transparency of qualifications and make credential evaluation easier (for higher education institutions and other stakeholders) and judgments more accurate;

- act as a common language/methodological approach that internationally can improve recognition and understanding between educational systems;

- facilitate the recognition of APEL and lifelong learning between states;

- simplify our understanding and improve the expression of the curriculum between countries through the use of common reference points;

- facilitate the application of the Lisbon Recognition Convention and the Code of Good Practice in the Provision of Transitional Education;

- enhance the precision of existing transparency instruments such as the Diploma Supplement;

- ease the pressure of work on the ENIC and NARIC Networks as well as individual centres;

- make ECTS, based on learning outcomes and levels, more effective as a credit system designed to promote access, flexibility and curriculum transparency (facilitating joint degrees);

- allow higher education institutes and credential evaluators to move away from imprecise measurement indicators that focus on formal procedures (admissions criteria, length of studies, qualification titles, years/hours of study undertaken) to focus on the results of student learning, and to move from input measurements to output/outcome measurements.

Problems and issues

Despite the optimistic picture presented above, qualifications frameworks will not work as a panacea solving all recognition problems. It must be stressed that the way forward is not simple or problem-free. Few countries have "new-style" qualifications frameworks and we must await the precise message in the Bergen Communiqué; the ministers in Bergen will have the final say.

The Bologna Process will certainly lead to greater mobility and more recognition problems. There are unresolved issues associated with the status of different length bachelor and master qualifications. ECTS has a major role to play in national and European qualification frameworks but it must be linked to levels and modules and courses would need to be expressed in terms of learning outcomes. Generally this is not the case at the moment.

The creation and acceptance of qualifications frameworks and the overarching framework for the European Higher Education Area cannot be achieved in a short time scale as both need the acceptance and active involvement of national and European stakeholders. Furthermore, the whole edifice depends on the creation and agreement of effective national quality assurance arrangements buttressed by autonomous higher education institutions that are accountable and responsible.

Concluding thoughts

The introduction of qualifications frameworks represents a series of challenges and opportunities to improve recognition. In theory, they have the potential to improve the clarity, accuracy and fairness of the recognition process. They can provide reference points against which clear decisions can be made. Increased transparency between national systems can lead to more trust and confidence. However, it will also provide real evidence of major differences in outcomes that may cause "zones of distrust". This is not necessarily a negative point as substantial differences between qualifications need to be acknowledged. There are a number of longstanding recognition problems that appear to defy resolution; frameworks and their associated methodological tools may help. The application of the Lisbon Recognition Convention should be made more effective. Qualifications frameworks could help to support a more constructive approach towards transnational education providers.

Recognition will remain an area where decisions are made by autonomous higher education institutions and other appropriate authorities. Qualifications frameworks and the framework for qualifications of the European Higher Education Area should be welcomed for the illumination they can provide to combat some of the academic prejudice that exists between different higher education institutions and between national education systems. Prejudice based on facts and information is preferable to prejudice based on custom and ignorance.

An intensive national and international dialogue should be encouraged to share good practice associated with the introduction of qualifications frameworks and their impact on recognition processes and issues.

International recognition and quality assurance – two priorities of the Bologna Process

Jindra Divis

Background

The national and international trends and developments in education which form the background to the Bologna Process are plain enough. Study programmes are becoming more diversified, not just as a result of the demand from students and society, but also because of the flexibility of supply on the side of the providers.

The qualifications and learning pathways are becoming increasingly individualised owing to a trend among providers towards more tailor-made approaches. Education is entering the virtual world, varying from the use of ICT to the creation of virtual universities. And whether you regard it as a part of the general trend towards globalisation or as a consequence of globalisation in the form of a conscious reply ("internationalisation"), there is no doubt that education is also going global.

There are many national and international responses to these trends and developments that go beyond the scope of this paper. Yet in a way, the culmination of these international responses is the Bologna Process. The Process represents the endeavours of 45 European countries to cope with the current international reality in the field of education. The Bologna Process is considered to be self-sustaining, with several actors providing the driving force. At international level, the European Commission has both the means and instruments to support the process, as well as an ambition to make the Process part of its economic strategy. Another body that supports the process is the Council of Europe, with its various networks and perspectives on higher education.

The main reason for the success of the Bologna Process so far is that the various parties at the national and international levels work together in a unique way. With the support of the various organisations, the basic principle is that what the national authorities agree upon at international level will find fertile soil at national level, and that the higher education institutions, students and other stakeholders will all play their role in implementing those principles. It goes without saying that both the rate of implementation and the level of enthusiasm do vary from country to country. Yet there is a general feeling that the Process represents an unprecedented reform of education on a huge scale, and one that most countries want to actively participate in.

The scope of this paper does not include a discussion of the general objectives and specific action lines that have already been detailed in the official documents: the Bologna Declaration itself (1999), and the Prague (2001) and Berlin (2003) Communiqués. I would instead like to focus on two lines of action: recognition and quality assurance.

One further issue that should be mentioned here, though, is the external dimension of the process. In the first stage, the focus was very much on the "Bologna area" itself. In the Berlin Communiqué, the outer world was rediscovered. Bologna would not only foster the appeal of European higher education, but it would also make Europe more open to co-operation. Especially from the point of view of the outside world, the issues of recognition of qualifications and quality assurance are of paramount importance.

Even in the Bologna Declaration, quality assurance was one of the main issues to be dealt with. The aim was that the relevant authorities in the field of quality assurance in Europe should co-operate closely in order to guarantee that the European Higher Education Area would be synonymous with high-quality – or even excellent – education. The main actor at international level is the European Network for Quality Assurance in Higher Education (ENQA). But ENQA is certainly not alone. Other organisations should also participate in the effort, in particular the European University Association (EUA) and the National Unions of Students in Europe (ESIB). Europe should enhance the culture of quality in its higher education institutions and endeavour to make its national systems as transparent as possible, so as to make the acceptance of other country's quality assessments or accreditation statements a feasible reality. The smooth recognition of diplomas and qualifications has become another objective of quality assurance in the international arena.

Although recognition was hardly even mentioned in the Bologna Declaration, the Prague Communiqué was already describing it as an important aspect of the Bologna Process and calling on the ENIC and

NARIC Networks[26] not only to get to work on matters of recognition, but also to establish contacts with the world of quality assurance, in other words with ENQA. The Berlin Communiqué of September 2003 went even further, making both recognition and quality assurance two of the three top priorities for the coming period (2003-2005):

> "Ministers charge the Follow-up Group with organising a stocktaking process in time for their summit in 2005 and undertaking to prepare detailed reports on the progress and implementation of the intermediate priorities set for the next two years: quality assurance, two-cycle system, recognition of degrees and periods of studies."

International recognition and quality assurance: where do they meet?

In general terms, quality assurance and accreditation have been set up for reasons of accountability, public protection and quality improvement. These are the objectives in the *national* setting. But safeguarding the quality of higher education qualifications is, of course, also a major concern of the system. In that respect, we might assume that the cross-border recognition of higher education qualifications is actually the most important objective of quality assurance in the *international* setting. And, for that matter, it is the assessment of quality (at least basic quality) or an accreditation decision which is the first concern for international recognition in assessing a qualification, whether for academic or for professional purposes.

It should be noted that the international recognition of qualifications is impossible without knowledge about the quality of the particular programme and the institution behind the qualification. Nor can it be granted on the basis of quality indicators alone. To assess a qualification fairly means to adequately position it in the grid of qualifications of the receiving country, and that requires a profound knowledge of the higher education system from which the qualification in question originates: apart from different quality of provision, qualifications with similar names coming from different countries may differ in their function in the national higher education system, admission and graduation requirements, planned learning outcomes as well as the professional status and

---

26. NARIC: the European Commission's network of National Academic Recognition Information Centres; ENIC: the Council of Europe and UNESCO/CEPES network of European National Information Centres on Recognition and Mobility.

title they give to the holder. But, again, the quality issue is of paramount importance from the perspective of recognition.

It is well known that quality assurance and quality accreditation are two different concepts in the approach to quality. However, in this paper they will be treated as one concept. The reason for this is that what is relevant from the point of view of international recognition is the *actual or final statement* about the quality of a programme or the institution teaching that programme, as stated by the competent authority of the national educational system. The concrete methodology, the specific infrastructure and the entire scope of objectives of the quality assurance and accreditation system are less important from this perspective.

At this juncture, one remark should be made about the notion or term "national". The assumption, as stated above, is that we deal with *national* systems of quality assurance or accreditation. The term refers to the authorities competent in this field in a country, without necessarily referring to the government or its involvement.

If there are no nationally sanctioned quality assurance or accreditation systems, the bodies involved in international recognition have a problem. The admissions officers or credential evaluators of the official recognition agencies – for example, in the field of regulated professions – base their evaluations on national laws and regulations, and on international agreements: in Europe, the Lisbon Recognition Convention[27] or the Directives of the European Union.[28] These legal instruments base their methodology on the existence of such national systems of quality assurance or accreditation. For example, the Lisbon Recognition Convention is applicable to qualifications awarded by institutions "belonging to a national education system". Today, it is difficult to see how this could be done without reference to quality assurance.

Students or employers outside the realm of the regulated professions may be less strict, but they too should strive for guaranteed quality. Alternative systems and mechanisms of quality assurance might be useful, especially in a field where national systems are not available, such as in the field of

---

27. The Convention on the Recognition of Qualifications concerning Higher Education in the European Region (Lisbon, 1997) may be found at: http://www.enic-naric.net/instruments.asp?display=legal_framework.
28. The EU Directives for professional recognition may be found at: http://europa.eu.int/comm/internal_market/qualifications/regprof/directives/dsp_directives.cfm.

non-degree programmes in most countries. But any quality assurance system which is not backed by the competent authorities is very difficult for outsiders to assess. Would-be students in particular should be very careful when making a deliberate choice to study at an institution which does not take part in some sort of national system of quality assurance or accreditation.

Coming back to the outputs of the national systems of quality assurance and accreditation, we can observe that defining and explaining such a quality statement within the national setting might be easy. To explore this subject in the cross-border context is a much more intricate matter. In the first place, the information and the channels carrying that information are not always available and sufficiently transparent to the public. Furthermore, in many cases the information and the information channels available are not "designed" to answer questions from a variety of stakeholders. Especially in the area of professional recognition – that is, recognition for the labour market – experience tells us that providing information about quality and quality assurance systems across borders does need an intermediary.

Problems in assessing foreign credentials arise because of a lack of clarity as to whether quality has been observed and/or guaranteed. And, if it has, how? Transnational or cross-border education falls within this area. With this, I mean education that cannot be traced back to a single national system. A similar problem arises with the joint curricula or joint degrees offered by higher education institutions in different countries, some of which belong to the national system of education, while others may not. In any case, even when institutions do belong to the national system of education, the matter is still not necessarily clear-cut. Many national quality assurance and/or accreditation systems are not accessible to these initiatives and so joint curricula and joint degrees fall outside these systems. Recognition across borders of joint degrees is an intricate matter, although these very initiatives should be considered prototypes of academic recognition in practice!

Similar problems arise in the field of distance learning and virtual education when these types of education do not belong to any national quality assurance and/or accreditation system.

The same applies for the concept of lifelong learning (LLL). The question of guaranteeing the quality of learning within the concept of LLL is a fundamental issue for the international recognition of the credentials concerned. Issues like learning outcomes and competencies, embedded in qualifications frameworks, and guaranteed through quality assurance provisions, are on the agenda of both recognition and quality assurance.

In general, both the fields of quality assurance and international recognition are being confronted with the same trends and developments in education and are having to deal with new education providers and new forms of education (and learning!). The Bologna Process "only" reinforces these developments and makes finding solutions more urgent, in particular thanks to its emphasis on *international employability*.

Certain issues of relevance to both concepts can be addressed in the traditional forms of higher education systems. The tendency to describe educational courses more and more in terms of "learning outcomes", or even in terms of competencies or competency profiles, and the increased co-operation in matching these profiles with those used by professional organisations or even industry, might be a field of common interests for quality assurance and recognition.

International initiatives

In the *national* setting, Bologna has strengthened the position of the institutions involved in recognition in many countries. Although the authorities have come to realise the role of recognition in the whole process, this has happened only after some hesitation. The idea was that comparable degrees and co-operation in quality assurance would result in the automatic recognition of credentials. No more recognition centres and networks! No more official structures and bodies for recognition! However, many practitioners and policy makers soon realised that this was not going to happen. In the first place, it takes a long time to achieve the desired level of co-ordination between the various systems of quality assurance. And, paradoxically, having comparable national degree structures is leading to an even greater diversification in the qualifications being awarded by competing education providers. We will continue to have a considerable diversity of profiles, but this diversity will be within a more clearly defined overall qualifications framework which, while not doing away with the need to assess individual qualifications, should make assessment easier and more transparent.

In most countries, the topic of quality assurance and accreditation received even more attention than it had in the previous decade, when this theme had already been identified as a priority. However, it is not possible within the scope of this chapter to elaborate on this issue.

In the *international* setting, the themes mentioned in the previous paragraph provide the joint agenda of the initiative of ENQA and the NARIC and ENIC Networks to work together. In more concrete terms, this is about developing a common language (for example, a joint glossary), about the question of how to deal with joint curricula and joint degrees, and about cross-border education. It is also about the development of a joint information provision system on quality assurance and accreditation to foreign target groups by the co-operating national recognition and quality assurance/accreditation institutions.

As stated above, the ENIC and NARIC Networks will have to develop more intense contacts with the EUA and ESIB, two key promoters of the culture of quality assurance in institutions in Europe. It should be said, however, that representatives of both organisations already attend the annual meetings of the networks. The EUA,[29] the largest European association of higher education institutions, is also concerning itself with the recognition of qualifications, as evidenced for instance by its co-ordinating role in ECTS and the Diploma Supplement in the recent past. It has also co-ordinated research, such as the studies on the introduction of bachelor's and master's degrees in Europe and the problem of joint degrees. This organisation's work most certainly straddles the boundary between recognition and quality assurance.

Another relevant quality assurance project from the perspective of recognition is the Joint Quality Initiative. This is an informal network, consisting mainly of representatives of quality assurance organisations and ministries, that aims to increase the transparency of collaboration between quality assurance systems, and to clarify the bachelor's/master's structures in Europe.[30] Its most important output is probably the "Shared descriptors for bachelor's and master's degrees" (the so-called "Dublin descriptors"), whereby generic learning objectives or competencies are set out for bachelor's and master's programme.

We should also mention at this point UNESCO's European higher education organisation, CEPES, in Bucharest.[31] This organisation, which acts as co-secretariat of the ENIC network alongside the Council of Europe,

---

29. http://www.unige.ch/eua/
30. http://www.jointquality.org
31. http://www.cepes.ro/

is also active in the field of accreditation with its "Indicators for Institutional and Programme Accreditation in Higher/Tertiary Education" project, part of "Strategic Indicators for Higher Education in the Twenty-first Century". A working group has analysed the quality indicators recently used in accreditation, searching for a set of core standards and corresponding performance indicators for both programme and institutional accreditation.

Three other ventures should be mentioned which, although they cross the boundaries of the Bologna zone, are still very important in bringing quality assurance and recognition together.

An initiative launched by UNESCO in October 2002 – the Global Forum for Quality Assurance, Accreditation and the Recognition of Diplomas[32] – is also an important development in bringing quality assurance and recognition together. Its aim is to place and maintain issues concerning quality assurance and the accreditation of programmes (or institutions) and the international recognition of diplomas on the agenda of the higher education sector and national and international policy makers.

Cross-border education receives particular attention from UNESCO. In 2004, UNESCO and the OECD initiated a new project entitled "Guidelines for quality provision in cross-border higher education". Its objective is to provide guidelines for all the relevant national stakeholders on how to deal with the issue of cross-border education provision. Part of this initiative involves setting up a database to connect the various national information channels on recognised higher education. This initiative was launched at the beginning of 2004 and will be finalised in the course of 2005.

Another international initiative is the International Network of Quality Assurance Agencies in Higher Education (INQAAHE).[33] The main aim of this network is to gather and disseminate information on existing and forthcoming quality assurance methodologies and practices in higher education. The idea behind this is to promote best practice in quality assurance and quality improvement. Its network function is very important, as it provides a place where quality assurance and accreditation organisations can meet, in both the literal and figurative sense of the word. INQAAHE also aims to foster the use of credit transfer systems and encourage institutions to provide material to facilitate the international recognition of diplomas. The network also intends to sound the

---

32. http://www.unesco.org/education/studyingabroad/highlights/global_forum_main.shtml
33. http://www.inqaahe.nl

alarm on any dubious accreditation processes and organisations, an activity which will be highly important for recognition.

Conclusion

Quality assurance and accreditation and the international recognition of qualifications have been seen to be two sides of the same coin. This idea, for some time promoted by experts from both fields, was endorsed by the European policy makers in the Berlin Communiqué.

The international educational community realises that both fields will promote the basic objectives of the Bologna Process, creating a true educational area with a strong mobility of students and professionals. They will do this not just in their own right, but increasingly in combination with each other. It is up to the experts in both fields to live up to the expectations and to make their contribution to the Bologna Process.

Recognising learning outcomes

Norman Sharp

Introduction

This paper will deal with the three main issues:

- What are learning outcomes?

- What is the state of development in learning outcomes across the Bologna countries?, and

- What difference will the adoption of learning outcomes make to the Bologna Process?

This chapter provides a very brief overview of some of the issues: it is neither intended to be an exhaustive nor a detailed technical analysis of learning outcomes. There are many references through which to pursue these matters and some of them are actually quite informative and interesting. There was an excellent presentation by Stephen Adam [2] on learning outcomes at a previous Bologna seminar in Edinburgh in July 2004. I would also commend the comments of Andrejs Rauhvargers [1] in his chapter in this book. In addition I would also recommend the excellent books by John Biggs [3] and by Paul Ramsden [4].

There is nothing difficult, mysterious or indeed particularly technical about learning outcomes. Thinking about learning outcomes provides us with an opportunity to look at pedagogical and learning and assessment processes using a particular lens – it is a lens which is frequently used by academics in certain contexts but laid aside in other contexts. The general thrust of my argument is that we need to encourage academics, students and others to use this lens more frequently and more systematically.

There are many reasons for adopting learning outcomes, some of which will be referred to in this paper. It seems that one of the most powerful reasons for thinking about learning outcomes is that their careful application can lead to a much improved pedagogical practice in higher education. Enhancing the student learning experience across the Bologna communities, and our influence on that experience, seems to be among the best of reasons, if not the very best reason, for devoting attention to learning outcomes. Because this is so important, I would like to dwell, just briefly, on the link between learning outcomes and pedagogical practice.

John Biggs [3] refers to the importance of reflective teaching in higher education. In his analysis he emphasises the importance of supporting students in the development of appropriate learning strategies. He draws the interesting analogy between teaching and fishing. It is all too easy, he argues, to approach students in higher education – perhaps through giving standard lectures and unimaginative seminars – as passive recipients of information. This kind of strategy is liable to produce students and graduates who are effective at absorption: at listening, processing and reproduction with perhaps precious little actually happening at the processing stage unless we are very careful. Biggs argues that such approaches are similar to providing fish for a single meal. Rather, he argues, we should support the development of the reflective practitioner. This, he argues, would be akin to supporting the development of the ability to fish for life.

This general approach of Biggs and others derives from the perspectives of constructivism: that is, in higher education it is our task to assist students to construct knowledge, and to construct that knowledge in meaningful frameworks. This very quickly takes us into a discussion of deep and surface approaches to learning which, will be touched on very briefly. These matters, however, are important – a surface approach to learning does not lead to the development of structured knowledge. It provides a disjointed array of outcomes. A deep approach yields meaning, at least as far as the student is concerned. Linked to this, I would in fact define good teaching as a teaching strategy that increased the probability of deep learning. In deep learning, knowledge is constructed by students in a personal way: it is created by the individual, not passively received from a transmitter.

If this is indeed how students learn effectively and construct knowledge, what does that imply for our approaches to teaching? The evidence points in this area to the importance of alignment – alignment of curriculum; teaching methods; assessment; climate of interaction with students; and, the whole institutional climate and sets of internal rules and procedures. With effective alignment, we can "entrap" students, as Biggs describes it, in "a web of consistency, optimising the likelihood that they will engage in appropriate learning activities but paradoxically leaving students free to construct their knowledge in their own way". This constructive alignment makes students do the real work of learning in higher education: the teacher acting as a broker between the student and the learning environment which is required to support effective learning activities.

In all of this, the fundamental building block on which almost all else is based is the concept of learning outcomes. It is through learning outcomes that students can be made aware of what the targets of learning are, and they are thus enabled to direct their activities towards achieving these outcomes. It is through the transparent sharing of these outcomes that all involved in assessment processes, including, perhaps most importantly the students, can devise and engage with appropriate assessment instruments: instruments that support learning and are actually meaningful in terms of providing valid and reliable information about the achievement of outcomes. It is through the explicit identification of learning outcomes that we can share knowledge about what is happening in the higher education systems of different countries. In the absence of the identification of learning outcomes, students are kept in the dark, institutions are kept in the dark and other countries in the Bologna area are kept in the dark. If we are all kept in the dark there can be no real sharing of assurance of quality and standards in relation to awards achieved or to comparability of processes. To conduct the debate in terms other than outcomes, such as duration of programmes, appears to be absolutely sterile: to know that a student has studied for five years tells us very little, if anything: to know that a student has achieved an identified set of learning outcomes which have been assessed in a valid and reliable manner, tells us a great deal. It is through the systematic application of learning outcomes that the Bologna Process will deliver its ultimate objectives.

What are learning outcomes?

We could spend many hours discussing the definition of learning outcomes. Learning outcomes have suffered in the past (and still do in some contexts) from a rather bad press:

– they are seen as reductionist and anti-higher education;

– they are confused with early work on competence;

– they were initially promoted by zealots with a somewhat narrow and functional educational perspective;

– they are viewed as focusing on the mediocre rather than the excellent.

I hope that the above comments will at least encourage colleagues to reflect on the real value of learning outcomes in addressing the interests of the students and other stakeholders that we are all here to serve. Their adoption is fundamental to the Bologna Process: why?

- the alternative input measures are unhelpful;

- they provide vital information to the student, employer, other institutions, professional and statutory bodies – nationally and internationally;

- they support mobility both of people and credit;

- they support desired pedagogical development – from teacher-centred to learner-centred;

- they support individuals in relation to wider access and lifelong learning through enabling the recognition, for example, of vocational education and training, work-based learning, and so on.

Without the adoption of learning outcomes the Bologna lines will remain largely lines on the page rather than lines of action and reality. In the absence of learning outcomes, I would argue, it will be very difficult to achieve readable and comparable degrees; the establishment of an effective system of credit within the Bologna area; mobility of the labour force or students; transparent assurance of quality and standards; or the geographically flexible pattern of lifelong learning envisaged in the Bologna Process.

What is the state of development in learning outcomes across the Bologna countries?

Stephen Adam indicates that:

> "learning outcomes have achieved an exalted status by the ubiquitous number of references to them in conferences, official documents and communiqués. This is in stark contrast to the poor level of understanding associated with them and their relatively rare practical implementation across Europe. Detailed experience of learning outcomes is in fact limited to just a few countries at both the institutional and national levels. This gap presents a significant challenge to the Bologna Process, and even calls into doubt the full realisation of the European higher education area by 2010. This makes the need for a better understanding a priority." [2]

However, Stephen Adam does draw a more optimistic view in the conclusions that he draws from his informal survey of development of learning outcomes across Europe. He concludes that, in fact, there is considerable activity across Europe. Of the 29 countries that volunteered information, 28 indicated some activity. "Activity", however, might have included any kind of development, including perhaps the most abstract academic discussions. At least eight of the countries reported minimum development. Other countries reported advanced stages of development and/or implementation of learning outcomes at all levels of educational activity, including: Belgium (Flemish community), Denmark, Hungary, Ireland, Italy, Slovak Republic, Spain, Sweden and the United Kingdom. It is interesting to note that in many of these countries the learning outcomes activity was characterised by a bottom-up approach – that is, dispersed institutional interest as opposed to top-down policy-driven developments. However, in the majority of cases in the report (52%), there was a clear top-down, ministry-led, impetus for change often accompanied by institutional level activity. Several of the countries surveyed indicated that the efforts in relation to learning outcomes were specifically linked to the Bologna agenda and specifically to the Berlin reform agenda.

Stephen Adam also reports that implementation appeared to be taking place right across Europe without any strong geographical, political or educational pattern emerging. However, he emphasises that this movement was, in general, more advanced in parts of northern and western Europe. Another interesting finding from the survey was that, in a significant number of cases, the developments in relation to learning outcomes were in specifically vocational areas; directly in VET; or in the polytechnic equivalent sectors. In some of these cases, the more purely "academic" institutions remained relatively isolated from developments in learning outcomes. Perhaps the most disquieting outcome of Stephen Adam's survey, however, was his comment that in no cases were the learning outcomes initiatives overtly linked with the adoption of improved pedagogical approaches.

Stephen Adam concludes his survey, a conclusion I would strongly endorse, by emphasising the thirst he found for increased sharing of knowledge and understanding in relation to the application of learning outcomes. It appeared in his conversations round Europe, that colleagues were extremely keen to take forward developments in learning outcomes but felt they lacked the necessary apparatus. My principal thesis in this chapter is that the required apparatus is already in place and indeed is extremely simple. A great disservice has been done by the generation of unhelpful literature and unnecessary complications in the area of learning outcomes to which I referred earlier.

What difference will the adoption of learning outcomes make to the Bologna Process?

In this penultimate section I want to refer back very briefly, to emphasise the importance of learning outcomes for the Bologna Process. This can be stated briefly but its brevity belies its importance. In relation to almost all the Bologna lines, further progress will not be made in the absence of learning outcomes. The alternative to using learning outcomes is almost always to use input measures: frequently input measures of time and other curriculum inputs. We are all familiar with the fact that students of literature may well study Shakespeare plays at elementary school, at high school, in college and university from undergraduate through to post-graduate levels, as well as in adult and community learning contexts. The fact that these texts are an input to the learning process in all of these different contexts tells us next to nothing about the outcomes achieved. What is important for the Bologna Process is to understand the outcomes achieved, not the inputs. If we do not understand the outputs we cannot begin to compare standards and quality across the Bologna countries. As was said earlier, it is a sterile debate to discuss the relative merits of standards or quality of programmes on the basis of time. To say a programme lasts five years tells us very little about what has been achieved over that five-year period. To avoid using learning outcomes is to avoid any real basis for comparison. If the European Higher Education Area is to become a reality, if the Bologna Process is to deliver what is expected of it, then learning outcomes have to be identified to allow effective comparability of quality and standards across many different kinds of programmes across the Bologna countries. In a similar vein, learning outcomes are required in order to provide appropriate information to students graduating from programmes; to universities accepting students on to programmes; to professional bodies certifying graduates as being competent; and, to employers employing graduates.

The Bologna Process is fundamentally about flexibility and mobility. Learning outcomes are essential to underpin student mobility and flexibility. A key tool to deliver all of this is an effective credit system. Without learning outcomes, the ECTS system will remain largely ineffective. It is absolutely essential that ECTS benefits from the experience of those qualification frameworks and credit structures that are based more soundly on learning outcomes. As I said earlier, the Bologna Process relies on the recognition of learning from a whole variety of different sources, and indeed that is the key raison d'être of a credit system. Through an effective credit system we will be able to link processes of recognition of prior learning, work-based learning, vocational education and training (VET) and academic credit within a single transparent framework. In the absence of the adoption of learning outcomes, this will simply not happen. Most importantly of all, however, as I tried to emphasise in my introduction, the real value of learning outcomes to the

Bologna Process is the support of effective pedagogical practice throughout the Bologna area. The adoption of learning outcomes is in my view a necessary precondition of the development of effective learning strategies in higher education. The adoption of learning outcomes and the constructive alignment that is built on the use of learning outcomes will support us in sustaining deep learning structures in the students we all seek to serve in all Bologna countries.

Some closing thoughts

Some closing thoughts that were further developed at the conference:

- without learning outcomes, the Bologna Process will have limited success;

- without learning outcomes, credit frameworks will be largely inoperable;

- without learning outcomes, some students will remain marginalised and immobile;

- without learning outcomes, approaches to learning in higher education will be less effective;

- we need now in the European Higher Education Area to build on a good start – there are no quick fixes.

References

1. Andrejs Rauhvargers (2004). *Improving the recognition of qualifications and study credit points.* Background report for the Bologna Process seminar on recognition, Riga, December 2004.

2. Stephen Adam (2004). *A consideration of the nature, role, application and implications for European education of employing learning outcomes at the local, national and international levels.* The United Kingdom Bologna Process seminar, Heriot-Watt University, Edinburgh, Scotland. July 2004, web address:
   http://www.bologna-bergen2005.no/EN/Bol_sem/Seminars/040701-02Edinburgh/040620LEARNING_OUTCOMES-Adams.pdf

3. John Biggs (2003). *Teaching for quality learning at university.* The Society for Research into Higher Education and Open University Press, London.

4. Paul Ramsden (2002). *Learning to teach in higher education*, Routledge, London.

Recognition of credits –
Achievements and challenges

Volker Gehmlich

"One of the objectives of the Bologna Action Plan is to launch a credit system, such as ECTS. The European Commission first introduced ECTS in 1989 as a transfer system and initiated its development into an accumulation system in the mid-1990s. ECTS was given real impetus when referred to in the Bologna Declaration and also when the European Universities Association agreed on the key features at the Zurich Conference in 2002. The Berlin Conference in 2003 confirmed the positioning of ECTS as a key element in the Bologna Process. In the following the achievements of introducing the system in all participating countries will be highlighted but so are the challenges which still have to be dealt with in the near future to make ECTS *the* successful "euro" in education and training."

The essential question is how achievements in the European Credit Transfer System (ECTS) can be quantified and qualified. It is proposed to identify those factors which are critical as regards the successful launch and implementation of ECTS. The critical success factors are *suitability* – is ECTS suitable for the purpose defined? *acceptability* – is ECTS acceptable for the stakeholders affected? feasibility – can ECTS be introduced at all? and finally *sustainability* – is such a system sustainable over a long period? is ECTS "fit for life"?

Critical success factor 1: Suitability – is ECTS fit for its purpose?

Credits document the achievement of learning objectives. These objectives are defined as learning outcomes by the designer of the respective module. Credits, being allocated to the learning outcomes of a module, highlight the expected notional workload the learner should invest. The common denominators are workload and learning outcomes. This is one of the outcomes of the project "Tuning educational structures in Europe", and has generally been accepted, so that ECTS is suitable to this extent.

Another issue is whether ECTS supports "employability" of higher education graduates, a cornerstone of the Bologna Declaration. The learning outcomes are developed on the basis of information from the labour market. How this information is acquired may differ from institution to institution. The "Tuning" project chose a questionnaire sent to employers, graduates and academics. It may be argued whether this is the best method as possible answers were predefined. But it can easily be amended by including other research methods as well, such as interviewing experts, analysing the technical press, or observing the labour market and so on. In this way learning outcomes are derived from the labour market. Before the learning outcomes are designed into programmes, academics have to scrutinise them in the light of long-term objectives, as information from the labour market is much more short-term oriented. Graduates and employers, for example, are much more concerned with their immediate situation.

The "Tuning" project has shown that agreement across universities in many countries can be achieved and that learning outcomes can be categorised into subject-related and non-subject-related (generic) competencies which the student acquires when having achieved specified learning outcomes. As a further subdivision it is possible to distinguish between broadening and widening of subject-related knowledge and understanding and generic learning outcomes making it possible to access knowledge and understanding. The latter are instrumental, interpersonal and systemic competencies. Each institution can even subdivide these competencies further according to its individual school of thought. The main message from "Tuning" is that the learning outcomes reflect the competencies necessary in the labour market and ECTS supplies an indication of what the notional workload is to achieve. Of course, it is then the decision of teaching staff how to translate these intended outcomes into modules, study programmes and so on. This shift of paradigm, from an input to an outcome orientation related to employment has been made very clear and is generally agreed.

The instruments of ECTS indicate how the success of quantified learning outcomes can be completed: the Information Package, Learning Agreement, Transcript of Records, the Credit Transfer and Accumulation and finally the Diploma Supplement document the processes which become transparent and that may thus be quality assured. By designing descriptors of levels – bachelor, master, doctor – "Tuning", the "Joint Initiative" (Dublin Descriptors) and soon the Qualifications Framework will mirror the competencies the labour market and the society needs today and tomorrow. The Information Package, containing all modules of respective programmes of institutions, details corresponding learning outcomes in the various modules and – by allocating ECTS credits – provides information about the notional workload the learner should invest. Thus effectiveness and efficiency of learning can be measured. If this equation is accepted one has to realise that higher education institutions will look much more strictly at their selection methods to make sure that they get those students who will be in a position to acquire the competencies within the time envisaged. Countries in which institutions may currently pride themselves on having high quality on the basis of high failure rates of learners may find themselves being regarded as outsiders as the question may be raised about whether they were not able to select those students who could be successful. In the future, good quality will be measured by "success rates" rather than by "failure rates" which will include "survival" in the labour market through close contact with alumni.

However, a credit system should not be limited to formal learning only. It should cover any form of learning, including non-formal and informal learning, which also means ultimately that a successful credit system should cover all forms of education and training, irrespective of where and how competencies are acquired.

The vocational training field is currently working on the launch of a credit system which is specifically designed for this form of learning: ECVET, a European credit system for vocational education and training in the light of the Bruges-Copenhagen Process. This is being done quite independently of the discussion going on within ECTS. It could be argued whether this is useful. Hopefully, this system will converge with ECTS and not develop independently. Again, the Qualifications Framework may forge an adequate approach.

Some countries already have a long-standing experience as regards the accreditation of prior learning and prior experiential learning. If my information is correct, one French university awarded a degree to a student who had never formally studied at that university. However, it was obviously possible to assess the student's prior learning and identify the level of the acquired learning outcomes as being equivalent to those of the degree awarded. Currently, some European projects are trying to find a solution which all institutions could apply, namely the project "ELITE

LLL" in which the ECTS label-holding institutions intend to develop ECTS as a system which can cover any area of education and training. There is some work in progress. The challenge is to design one credit system for all learning and training purposes, for a lifelong concept.

Critical success factor 2: Acceptability – is ECTS fit for stakeholders?

To find out whether ECTS fulfils this critical success factor, it has to be identified whom ECTS serves. A credit system has to respect the perspectives of its stakeholders. In the case of ECTS these must be the learners first of all but also training and teaching staff and employers. But there are others as well who have to be considered, the parents, governments, social partners and finally society as a whole. Stakeholders may argue in terms of their *return* or *risk* when using ECTS. They may "make or break" ECTS as an overarching credit system for teaching and training depending on their interest and power.

In *return* the learner receives a number of credits. These credits reflect a value which is expressed by learning outcomes – that is, the competencies the learner has acquired after having proved that he or she has acquired these competencies successfully. Credits are only awarded when this process has taken place, regardless of how the learner achieved the competencies.

The *risk* is related to the recognition of the credits in the event that they are submitted to a teaching, training or business organisation and so on. Is the number of credits being accepted identical to the number submitted to the institution; are there more or fewer credits being taken into account? Within ECTS it is the responsibility of the "receiving institution" to make a decision as regards the number of credits being accepted. Its decision will be based on the programme for which the credits will be recognised. The risk is that the number of credits transcribed will not be identical to the number received from the institution which awarded them. In fact, if this were the case it would be by accident only, unless all institutions in Europe had agreed on an identical number of credits per module to be proposed as "good practice". This, however, is no shortcoming of ECTS; in fact it proves that ECTS is working, that credits cannot be accepted blindly but have to be considered on the basis of the learning outcomes in respect of the learning programme for which they are considered.

Stakeholder mapping not only reflects the stakeholders' expectations but also their power to influence the launch of ECTS as *the* credit system. The mapping helps to find out which stakeholders should be considered first of all, for example accreditation agencies or quality assurance agencies and so on, when a tuned system has been introduced across Europe. Also, the Bologna Process as such, in particular in terms of the decision on whether the European Qualifications Framework will be based on both learning outcomes and respective credits, is a stakeholder in terms of those who design it. They have both interest and power. It could be argued that learners, teachers and employers are the key players. To a certain extent this is correct; they surely have a high interest in the development. The question remains whether they also have the power to launch ECTS Europe-wide. It should be noted that without their understanding and support, the sustainability of ECTS would suffer and would – most likely – be deemed to have failed.

Since the development from a transfer to an accumulation system there has been an increase of interest in the expectations but also an understanding as regards possible risks. In contrast to the 1990s it is now obvious that there are some stakeholders who do not only have the interest but also the power "to make it happen" – if they want to.

Critical success factor 3: Feasibility – fit to live?

ECTS is the only system which has been tested successfully Europe-wide. A feasibility study at the beginning of the 1990s revealed that it was possible to develop ECTS from a transfer system to a transfer and accumulation system. This has been initiated and the developments in the Bologna member states provide sufficient evidence that ECTS today is an adequate credit system. Guarantors for the launch are the bodies which design the European Quality Assurance System, the accreditation and evaluation bodies at national level and the European Qualifications Framework, based on learning outcomes and credits. In other words, ECTS links the priorities for the next Bologna ministerial meeting in Bergen in May 2005, namely quality assurance, an overarching qualifications framework and academic recognition.

Critical success factor 4: Sustainability – fit for life?

To launch ECTS as the European credit system is one thing, to keep it alive another. Within the European context an immediate idea is that in education and training credits should become a currency, a kind of euro. Could ECTS be such a currency? Does a credit in the ECTS system fulfil similar objectives to those of the euro – in other words, does it comprise the basic elements of a currency which:

– is based on trust;

– is generally accepted;

– works as a unit of account;

– respects convertibility;

– enables recognition;

– represents value;

– is convertible; and

– is compatible (a common reference)?

The Key Features of ECTS give an indication: "... one credit stands for 25-30 hours of working" and "Student workload in ECTS includes the time spent in attending lectures, seminars, independent study, preparation for, and taking of, examinations, etc.". Technically speaking, the introduction of ECTS as a currency is no problem.

Does everybody trust that the number of "units of account", credits, is adequately allocated? As soon as the credit is intended to be used outside the area where they were gained, problems come up. The reason is that a unit of account does not only have to do with quantity. There must be a certain value behind it in which people believe and which they regard as being adequate in relation to the number of credits in question. In ECTS the value of a credit is the learning outcome related to it. This is made transparent. At the same time, however, this also indicates the borderline of a credit system. The value may change as soon as the environment in which the credit was achieved is changed. This is comparable to the European Monetary Union. The purchasing power of a euro is not only different outside the founding member states but also within them. The absolute, nominal value stays the same but the relative one, the market value, normally differs on account of purchasing power, which is the reciprocal value of the general price level. Within this context this refers to the acceptance of credits for specified learning programmes. In relation to the whole education and training area this means that credits acquired

86

may not be recognised for any learning programme in an identical way. Those responsible for a learning programme settle the question to what extent competencies acquired elsewhere can be considered relevant within their programme. Thus, ECTS does not lead to an automatic recognition of credits. The institution at which the learner applies to have the credits accepted autonomously forms its own opinion. This is quite normal in business as well: the salesperson decides whether the product or service is exchanged for a specified price. The potential buyer might bargain but cannot make the decision.

By analogy with the currency system, credits are a requirement for the principle of "division of learning" – that is, learning at different sites and at various times, in other words for a concept of lifelong learning. Credits may be awarded for any type of learning – formal, non-formal or informal. They may be accumulated in working towards particular degrees. Because of their relationship to the acquisition of knowledge and understanding on the basis of workload, they form a unit of account. Convertibility is possible on the basis of the parity generally accepted, the learning outcomes.

An example might help to state the case. The Common European Framework of Reference for Languages defines various levels of competence from A to C, each of them being subdivided. It is assumed that these levels build on each other, and that the higher the level, the higher a learner has progressed in language skills.

For the sake of the example it is anticipated that for achieving level B1 a workload of 900 hours were needed. In ECTS terms this means 30 credits. The question is: what can the learner do with the credits? If the intention is to reach the next stage, B2, these 30 credits should be the entry ticket for a corresponding formal programme. This means that the "full" 30 credits will be accredited and the prior learning should be recognised to the extent that the credits achieved testify to the level of the learning outcomes. Non-formal and informal learning are hardly applicable in this case as they are purely based on post-evaluation.

But what else can the learner "buy" for the 30 credits? If the intention is to study European business, a language might be an essential part of such programmes. Does this mean that the 30 credits count already towards the 180 of the bachelor's programme registered for? Hardly; it is obvious that as soon as the credits achieved are "traded in" for a defined learning programme, the absolute value of the learning outcomes acquired becomes relative. Only that number of credits can be recognised which is envisaged in the study programme and for which the learning outcomes have been defined. Maybe they are even below B1, for example at A2 level. It is obvious that it is nice to have a higher level but for the programme the value is limited, and therefore the number of credits required for A2 will be accredited. In another scenario it may be – and this is even likely in European business – that the learners of the language do not start from scratch; prior knowledge is a prerequisite. Again, the absolute 30 credits become relative and may be worth only 5 because of the notional workload reserved in this programme for reaching the language level the "newcomer" may already have.

In other words, ECTS credits are acquired in absolute terms. However, when the learner wants to use them the level for which he or she may obtain recognition differs, depending on the learning programme for which recognition is being sought. When measuring credits this distinction has to be very clear: absolute credits measure the workload, expressed in the notional time which has to be invested to reach these stand-alone subject-related or generic competencies. The absolute value of a credit is a value as such and might play a role when, for example, the holder of the credits applies for a given job and the potential employer asks for evidence of "what can you do?" or when he/she has to consider whether the applicant may be employable at all.

Is it possible to measure all subject and generic skills in absolute terms? It is highly likely but it means that experts have to put their heads together and work out proposals which then have to be validated in practice. "Tuning" could be an ideal test-bed for such competencies, at least for some. Also, some prior work has been done already: the European driving licence and many other programmes of teaching and learning have been designed over the years, covering subject and generic skills. These programmes should be systematically compiled to get an overall view. In other words, to get an understanding of measuring competencies the first thing is to identify their absolute value. And this can only be done by identifying the learning outcomes first. Also, this cannot be done by one person, let alone by one institution, be it a university or any other organisation. This is the job of specialists drawn from all areas concerned: teaching, training, education (educationalists), employers, researchers, trade union members, learners, and so on. Flexible working groups should draw up proposals which must be tested and empirical data has to be compiled. In many cases this can perhaps be done by secondary research, investigating the profiles of learners. This will be facilitated by the present discussion of standardising learning outcomes in countries in which they have not been identified yet. In some countries with national standards, it might be much easier to determine the workload for competencies and skills.

What one can take from this example is that the various levels should be designed to improve transparency of learning achievements. However, they should not represent a certain status as they should serve all qualifications. If they did, the system would get blocked and a "ladder" career would be created which would take away all mobility between various programmes. This is against the philosophy of ECTS as a credit system which seeks to foster mobility within and between learning programmes, within and between institutions and within and between different countries.

Thus, in contrast to the European Framework of Reference for Languages, the levels in an overarching European Qualifications Framework do not represent a status, they define learning outcomes for which credits are allocated to inform us what we have attained with what notional workload. Again, if these credits are traded in, it may mean that the learner starts at a different level because the programme he or she has registered for is designed differently. If this were not the case the impression would be given that learning is always a steady upwards curve in a given subject or generic area. The reality, however, is much more complex and thus different levels of subject and generic skills may well be combined to be eligible for a certain degree in various environments. Thus, levels do not award status but have an impact on pursuing activities in differing environments, at school, university or employment, and so on. Also, if this were not the case, several credit systems would soon be created, being explained on the basis of levels: bachelor's credits, master's credits, school credits, and so on. Goodbye to any attempt to achieve a cohesive European credit system.

Does this lead to standardised study programmes? Not necessarily, unless the stakeholders think this is desirable in particular subject areas (for example, joint degrees, or the Euro-Bachelor in Chemistry). Instead, the introduction of an education and training "euro" forms a key requirement of lifelong learning concepts. Such a currency is geared towards learners, values, competencies and employability.

Conclusion

ECTS as a transfer and accumulation system has unintentionally basically been designed as a currency system. All aspects related to a currency system are therefore valid for ECTS as well. This relates, for example, to issues such as:

- "purchasing power" of the outcomes;
- conversion of achievements at institutional, national and international level;
- fluctuations of values;
- formal, non-formal and informal achievements.

As with any currency, the basic element today is trust. How can this be achieved for ECTS? As in the monetary union, stability criteria have to be adhered to first of all. For education and training this means quality in terms of:

- transparency;
- tuned structures, processes and products.

Thus, the challenge for Bologna in 2007 will be to design one currency: ECTS. This seems to be the only way to achieve the objectives relating to the intention of the Bologna Process. Everybody will understand: a credit is a credit, just as a euro is a euro.

Developments along subject lines and their impact on recognition

Julia González and Robert Wagenaar

Introduction

Comparable degrees and fair recognition of periods of study taken abroad are at the very heart of the Bologna Process. In the emerging European Higher Education Area (EHEA) comparability and recognition are both linked to mobility. The learner of today and tomorrow increasingly expects to have the option to study and work in different countries without being bothered by recognition problems. This calls for effective, clear, comprehensive and rapid recognition systems, which fully take into account the quantity and quality of work done by the learner. It is obvious that a single European economic area cannot work well without having a single higher education area. This message has been understood by policy makers, recognition agencies, quality bodies and, above all, higher education institutions. The latter are crucial actors because it is ultimately the institutions that offer and award degrees. Degrees are always based on a subject area which can be broad or small and might have a monodisciplinary, multidisciplinary or interdisciplinary approach. Qualifications are offered in a particular cultural and educational setting in which national, local and institutional traditions play a role. These elements have to be taken into account when academic and professional recognition are concerned. This paper focuses on ways which have been developed to simplify and improve recognition from the perspective of higher education institutions and especially subject areas.

Improvement of recognition starts with a language which is commonly understood by those involved in recognition matters. Developing such a language requires platforms to get acquainted with the different ways in which subject areas are taught and learned within and outside Europe. Although a number of very useful tools have been developed by organisations such as ENIC-NARIC, a real common language is not yet in existence. The Bologna Process has been helpful in promoting the need for this language. The process, being built on the notion of consensus, has stimulated the convergence of European educational systems by introducing a three-cycle system. This in itself has facilitated processes of recognition. Also, there has been the important role of Socrates thematic networks, which during the past decade have led to a better understanding between experts at disciplinary level from the different European countries. These initiatives, together with international staff and student mobility as well as transnational curriculum development, have contributed to the growing EHEA.

The creation of such an EHEA has never been perceived as a process of homogenisation and it is important to stress that it should not. One of the selling points of European higher education in a global context today is its cultural diversity and richness. It is one of the main features which has created its identity. It is this variety that favours increasing co-operation and competitiveness, which are both high on the European agenda. Having said this, it shows at the same time the necessity to have reliable and transparent mechanisms for organising recognition, probably even more so for Europe than for other regions.

Given the importance of diversity, transparency tools are required which cover the whole recognition system. The days of partial recognition of degrees and "ad hoc" ways of recognising periods of studies should be over. The challenge for today and tomorrow is to be able to recognise periods of study in a systematic, comprehensive and well-accepted manner, taking into account different cultural and academic contexts and qualifications. This means that we should no longer base recognition on course unit to course unit comparison, with the intention of replicating the elements of the local degree. Instead we should focus on more general basic assumptions such as credits and learning outcomes. For this approach different initiatives have been taken, of which the most important are the *European Credit Transfer and Accumulation System* (abbreviated as ECTS), a *Framework for Qualifications of the European Higher Education Area* (EFQ) and the project *Tuning Educational Structures in Europe* (Tuning Project). These are powerful tools and systems in themselves, which respond to different needs and purposes.

ECTS relates to both the overall degree programme and the small units of learning of which a programme consists, looking at their nature and seeing them in the context of achievement of outcomes and progress towards the degree. A European credit system which is built on agreed approaches to information exchange, learning agreements and transcripts of records goes beyond mobility *pur sang*. Such a transparency system is also a crucial tool for programme design and programme recognition covering both transfer and accumulation of learning. It offers flexibility and understanding for a particular programme and its specific building blocks. Probably the most important element of ECTS is that it calls for detailed reflection on the workload of a typical student required to achieve particular outcomes.

As a transparency tool, the EFQ is crucial for recognition as:

"an overarching framework that makes transparent the relationship between European national higher education frameworks of qualifications and the qualifications they contain. It is an articulation mechanism between national frameworks".

This presupposes the existence of national frameworks where:

"all qualifications and other learning achievements in higher education may be described and related to each other in a coherent way and which defines the relationship between higher education qualifications".[34]

This articulation of the system at both national and European level is of the greatest importance. Since degrees are recognised firstly at national level, the location of a qualification in the national qualifications framework is of the greatest significance. It is ultimately the national authorities which will recognise and to that end will be helped by the understanding gained through the overarching qualifications framework.

Recognition along subject area lines

Besides credit and qualification systems there is another, complementary, perspective towards recognition. This perspective takes into consideration the academic and professional communities related to the subject area. This reference is global by nature, although a level of specificity and articulation is possible at European and even at country level. Some countries have developed a benchmarking system; others have core concepts and descriptors in their regulations.

In the academic year 2000-2001, a group of over one hundred European universities initiated the Tuning Project. This project is a response by the academic community to the Bologna Process. The main objective is to develop jointly a system which makes degree programmes comparable, compatible and transparent and by doing so responds to the demands of the European Higher Education Area. This initiative treats in a co-ordinated manner the need for a system based on the disciplinary perspective. It has obtained the full support of the European Commission, which considers it "at the heart of the Bologna Process since it addresses several of

---

34. Bologna Working Group on Qualifications Frameworks, report on "A European Framework for Qualifications of the European Higher Education Area" (Copenhagen, February 2005).

its lines of action: easily readable and comparable degrees, adoption of a system of credits, quality enhancement".[35]

At the beginning of 2003 Tuning published its first report. It reflects the results of its first phase, in which it focused on the development of internationally understood reference points for subject specific competencies (knowledge, understanding and skills) and generic competencies, and the further development of ECTS into an accumulation system based on learning outcomes expressed in terms of competencies as well as credits based on student workload. Since Tuning I, three main developments can be noticed:

– a substantial geographical expansion, which shows the growing interest, as well as the acceptance of its approach of a non-invasive nature and its adequacy to deal with different local contexts;

– the inclusion of further subject areas in the project; and

– the deepening and refinement of the project outcomes.

The rapidity of the geographical expansion can be seen as proof of the international appeal of subject-area "reference points" at the level of academic communities. Starting with higher education institutions in 16 countries – Austria, Belgium, Denmark, Germany, Finland, France, Greece, Iceland, Ireland, Italy, the Netherlands, Norway, Portugal, Spain, Sweden and the United Kingdom – the Tuning Project added during its second phase (2003-2004) institutions from another nine countries: Bulgaria, the Czech Republic, Estonia, Latvia, Lithuania, Poland, Romania, Slovenia and Slovakia.

In July 2004 Tuning America Latina was approved as an ALFA project. This showed the interest of universities on both sides of the Atlantic in exploring jointly degree profiles and competencies in consultation with their professional organisations and other stakeholders. Another 18 countries joined the project: Argentina, Bolivia, Brazil, Chile, Colombia, Costa Rica, Cuba, Ecuador, El Salvador, Guatemala, Honduras, Mexico, Nicaragua, Panama, Paraguay, Peru, Uruguay and Venezuela.

By the year 2005 universities from all the Bologna signatory countries have expressed their wish to be part of Tuning. Seven more European countries, including Switzerland and Ukraine, are expected to initiate the process in phase 3. The rest will probably follow soon. This means that there are, at present, participating universities from some fifty countries.

---

35. Commissioner Viviane Reding at the Closing Conference of Tuning I, 31 May 2002.

Other academic communities from other regions, such as Russia, Japan and India, have already shown their interest and preparations to include them in the process are under way.

The second line of development refers to the involvement of an increasing number of subject areas. The initial project started with seven: educational science, mathematics, business, history, geology (earth science), physics and chemistry. To these, nursing and European studies were added as examples of a regulated and a multidisciplinary subject area respectively.

On the initiative and with the support of the European Commission, the Socrates thematic networks began to explore the use of the Tuning methodology in their specific subject areas soon after the first phase of Tuning. By 2005 the majority of the Thematic Networks have co-operation links with Tuning that go beyond awareness and dissemination. An increasing number of networks are currently implementing the Tuning approach in their subject areas, such as occupational therapy, civil engineering, architecture, landscape education, medical studies, geography, the arts, music, electrical and information engineering, radiography, computing, dentistry, political sciences, geodetic engineering and food sciences. Some of these networks use the Tuning approach in the development of joint degrees, in particular in master's programmes. The co-operation with subject areas also includes European associations, for example the European Law Faculties Association (ELFA), which will develop the Tuning methodology in the field of legal studies.

This joint work includes the incorporation of new elements and good practices which have been developed over several years for the relevant academic communities and which seem to be particularly suitable for a well-defined subject area. This provides variety and richness to the European and international understanding of developments along thematic lines while maintaining a single approach and a general consistency. This allows the use of a referential language for common understanding beyond and across the subject areas.

It is expected that the work done in co-operation in order to develop representative platforms, prepare adequate consultation processes and define the related competencies and learning outcomes will include all the variety of the specific academic traditions. It is also expected that the results will be expressed in a systematic comparable manner, in a commonly understood language which will promote transparency and allow readability and comparison.

Besides the geographical expansion and the inclusion of further subject areas, the third development of Tuning follows the project's progression and the furthering of its outcomes. From the very start in 2000 a number of relevant elements were present:

— Awareness of the need for a tool for higher education institutions to be able to contribute to the creation of the European Higher Education Area. Such a tool for transparency should provide for a common approach along the different subject area lines. To develop this tool, it proved crucial to define the nature of degrees at first, second and third cycle at European level. But recognition and the creation of EHEA also required the development of a system where the thematic nature of the degrees became transparent, for each of the cycles.

— Awareness of a vision regarding education which linked employability with personal growth and citizenship in a knowledge-based society.

— Awareness of a shift of paradigm taking place in higher education towards output-based learning.

— Need for platforms of academics from different countries in the specific fields to debate and to reach agreements and shared understanding about key issues at subject area level.

— Relevance of a methodology for consensus building in relation to the Bologna degrees along subject lines. Key elements of this approach were identified as learning outcomes and competencies: generic and subject-specific competencies, agreed competencies used as reference points, and competencies identified in consultation with stakeholders. It was also obvious from the very start that the use of competencies would require new approaches to teaching, learning and assessment.

— Importance of student-centred learning, expressed in ECTS credits based on student workload and used in the design and delivery of the degree programme.

— Importance of introducing programme quality enhancement for programme design, as well as development and implementation.

Work done in Tuning I with regard to these elements was followed by further work on the refinement of the learning outcomes and competencies already identified, discussed and agreed. They were then read in the context of the newly created EFQ. In the process of further developing the

96

transparency tools, the ECTS system was renewed to relate to the learning outcomes and competency-based approach. Also, an approach was designed to measure student workload. Another direction of this process of development was provided by identifying a number of best practices in relation to learning, teaching and assessment of the jointly defined competencies. The outline of the Tuning methodology was thus completed for the design phase of degree programmes. In order to help rapid readability and comparison across subject areas, a template was created. The aim was to provide, in a very succinct manner, the basic elements for a quick introduction to a subject area.

While the EFQ helps to identify a degree in the EHEA through the national qualifications frameworks, Tuning, through the documents and templates devised and agreed by the European thematic communities organised into platforms, tries to facilitate the location of the degrees in a disciplinary context. What makes a first-cycle degree in history different from one in law or in physics? It is this identification which allows recognition not only as a first degree, but as a first degree in history, law or physics.

The template sets out to give details of the relevant issues in the specific subject area and the map of professions which are normally related to that area on the European scene. The Berlin Communiqué incorporated into the Bologna language a number of key instruments in the development of comparable degrees: profile, learning outcomes and competencies, level and student workload. These were considered by Tuning to be landmarks in programme design from the start of its project.[36]

The development of a degree profile takes place in the initial stages of degree planning. It relates to the need which has been identified and the potential which has been discovered. It connects directly with the origins of the programme and it is crucial for its understanding. In the EHEA it may be anticipated that there will be no two profiles which are equal to each other. There is not a single way of answering a need, not even of perceiving it. This is a sign of variety and innovation and it is important that this is maintained, emphasised and celebrated. The design, the development and the writing of a degree profile is the moment to determine the combination of elements which will give a particular degree its specific

---

36. Julia González and Robert Wagenaar, eds., *Tuning Educational Structures in Europe. Final Report. Pilot Project – Phase 1* (Bilbao-Groningen, 2003). More information about the Tuning project can be found on the following Internet sites:
http://europa.eu.int/comm/education/policies/educ/tuning/tuning_en.html and
http://tuning.unideusto.org/tuningeu/

identity mark – an interesting mixture of elements whereby the graduates of a particular department, university or degree will become identified.

When a new field of knowledge is initiated, degree profiles can be regarded as totally innovative. In such cases disciplinary references are sometimes very small, because these degrees are often interdisciplinary or multidisciplinary in nature and are therefore trend-setters to which others have to refer. However, existing degree programmes have normally proved their necessity for the development of society. Also with regard to those degree programmes, it continues to be the responsibility of the higher education institutions to educate citizens in the most intelligent, fair and innovative manner. Higher education institutions and subject-related academic traditions have the built-up knowledge and understanding to do so and to articulate the already existing knowledge in the field.

A consensus has emerged in Tuning regarding the tendency for degree profiles to diversify and to become more specific as they move upwards from first- to second-cycle degree level. These profiles relate to the widening, deepening and specialising of basic knowledge of the subject area. Sometimes, degrees are referred to as having a generalist or specific profile, a research profile or a professional profile and so on. This variety is to be kept:

–   provided it is articulated in a consistent manner at country and subject area level; and

–   provided that with the adequate tools for transparency the differences can be identified and recognition is made possible.

Degree profiles guide the choice of the learning outcomes and competencies used and developed in a particular programme. The higher education institution/department may have particular strengths or policies owing to a particular vision of the importance of educating a particular type of professional. In this sense the degrees will bear an identity mark referring to the place where they were granted. Degree profiles show that the combination of learning outcomes and competencies has a backbone that sustains it and makes it recognisable for what it is. There are elements in the profile that relate in a generic manner to other degrees which are located in the same cycle level in the Qualifications Framework: a level of development of the competencies of knowledge and understanding, the capacity to make informed judgments, to move from theory into practice, and levels of communication and of further learning. This is the contribution of the EFQ; Tuning provides the disciplinary context and articulation.

Degrees are located by co-ordinates relating to the nature of degree cycle – first, second and third cycle (vertical line) – and to subject area (horizontal line) expressed in terms of profiles, learning outcomes and competencies at discipline level.

The degree profile is closely related to the learning outcomes and competencies which constitute the hard core of a degree's identity. These are crucial for recognition. Here again choices ought to be made. Tuning has pointed to the fact that in an ever-changing society, with high mobility in employment, generic or transferable competencies are of great significance and every degree profile should make choices in relation to the more suitable ones in relation to the desired outcome of the programme. Tuning consulted graduates, employers and academics in a structured way to identify the most relevant generic competencies. The subject area groups agreed on the set of most important generic competencies for their field. What also became evident was that the consultation process regarding generic competencies, such as capacity for analysis and synthesis and problem-solving ability, showed interesting variations when it was applied, for example, to the subject area of physics, the context of law or the historical field.

In particular, the subject-related learning outcomes and competencies (knowledge, understanding, skills and abilities) should have a clear impact on the curriculum. Again there is plenty of room for a variety of paths and learning situations, taking into consideration that these need to be consistent with the degree profile and have an acceptable level of reference to what the academic community, in dialogue with the professional bodies, considers the "common" "identifying" elements. This minimum core will make a degree of mathematics identifiable, just as it will make a degree in nursing recognisable.

After intensive sessions of discussion based on careful listening to each other and understanding different approaches, the Tuning subject area groups were able to identify consensus with regard to what a student should know, understand and be able to do in terms of key learning outcomes to be achieved and key competencies to be obtained by the learner; these are crucial elements for recognition. Tuning offers a number of agreed learning outcomes and competencies for a growing number of subject areas. They are presented as reference points for the identification of the identity core in order to facilitate comparability and recognition.

A further element of analysis which is both present in the Berlin Communiqué and familiar to the tradition from which the Tuning initiative developed is the reference to ECTS credits based on student workload.

Tuning is convinced that defining a profile and agreeing on the basis of the learning outcomes of a degree programme as such is not sufficient. It is seen as an absolute necessity that the volume and weight of the programme correspond to the time available for the students to reach the learning outcomes. In other words, a programme of learning must be feasible within the given time frame. The use of ECTS credits not only facilitates this feasibility but also facilitates the consistency of the programme by linking desired outcomes with the weight given to the different elements of the programme.

Finally, there are two further items in the template: approaches to learning, teaching and assessment and quality enhancement. Teaching, learning and assessment methods and techniques are important pointers in the process of learning. They may affect the specificity of a particular degree programme in the sense that the nature and length of educational experiences can have an impact on the type of degree or even on its duration. Also, the reference to quality enhancement provides a dimension of the programme which has to be considered. The notion of quality assurance should be present during the whole process of designing, developing and implementing a degree programme.

To summarise, in the template degree profiles are limited to a typical degree of a concrete subject area. This is reflected in the learning outcomes and competencies. They should only be seen as reference points. The ECTS credits show the amount of time that would normally be required to meet the given learning outcomes. The item on learning, teaching and assessment provides space for reflection and programming, considering the best routes to attain the aims pursued. Quality enhancement is present in the template to raise the awareness of important developments in the field and to point to the importance of securing the need to consider how the consistency of the process can be guaranteed and internally checked.

Conclusions

As a result of the Tuning initiative, higher education institutions have responded to the Bologna challenge in a co-ordinated manner. The institutions involved have felt the need and responsibility to explore the development of the "new-style" degrees in order to facilitate recognition of degrees and periods abroad. Another new and important initiative which developed more or less during the same time at which Tuning was being devised is the Framework for Qualifications of the European Higher Education Area. Both initiatives seem to complement each other perfectly and are in accordance with tools that were developed earlier such as the ECTS, the Diploma Supplement or the EUROPASS.

A significant number of representatives from different higher education institutions, subject areas and countries identified the need for a system, a tool to facilitate recognition and to make possible and operational a number of the Bologna action lines which relate to the nature of comparable and readable degrees. They developed the Tuning Project in a process of consultation with stakeholders, consensus building and intellectual debate. They created a methodology to fill a clearly identifiable need.

The Tuning approach has proved to be non-invasive and seems to work well both at the level of subject area (in some twenty subject areas, with a growing number that wish to adopt the approach) and at country level (some 50 countries represented by institutions and academics are already involved, with an increasing number wishing to initiate the process). This means that the philosophy regarding education and the common language developed is understood and has meaning for them.

It may be said in conclusion that Tuning has succeeded in developing a methodology by using common key concepts and tools in constant dialogue with the different actors: learning outcomes and competencies, consultation with stakeholders, student-centred learning, workload, degree profiles, the use of reference points rather than norms or standards, mutual respect and recognition of the work being developed by other actors, co-operation and avoidance of duplication which might have led to confusion. A powerful tool has thereby been created which will prove to be an important contribution to the recognition of degree programmes and periods of study along the lines of subject areas.

Recognition in the labour market

Jindra Divis

Background

On 19 June 1999, 29 European ministers of education, meeting to sign the Bologna Declaration, called for the "adoption of a system of easily readable and comparable degrees... in order to promote European citizens' employability...". One feature of the proposed new degree structure was that the "degree awarded after the first cycle shall also be relevant to the European labour market as an appropriate level of qualification".

Does a European or even an international labour market exist? Or is it more appropriate to talk about national labour markets that have to cope with the growing mobility of capital and people? To defend the latter viewpoint, we would have to disregard the growing importance of globalisation in both labour and education, which is discernible everywhere. And certainly in the EU the "internal market" is an international one. In any case, in this chapter we shall go along with the generally accepted assumption that there is an international labour market. And this labour market has to take into account education in all its forms and locations. We shall be discussing human resource development and employability in the international context.

An international labour market requires a fair and effective mechanism to assess qualifications awarded in various countries and continents. In this chapter we will focus on the European situation, to outline relevant methodologies and procedures for recognition.

International recognition of diplomas and qualifications

Terminology

There are two types of international recognition of diplomas and qualifications, which require two types of credential evaluation: academic recognition and professional recognition.

Academic recognition refers to recognition decisions that allow a person to pursue or continue a course of study or confer the right to use a national title or degree from the host country on the basis of a title or degree acquired in the country of origin. One example would be using the Dutch *doctorandus* (drs.) title on the basis of a master's degree obtained in the US.

Professional recognition relates to the methodologies and procedures for evaluating credentials for work purposes and is a more intricate matter. The system of professional qualifications reflects both the national system of education and the organisation of professions, industries and professionals themselves. In some countries, such as Germany and the Netherlands, most academic qualifications also serve as professional qualifications without additional requirements. In other countries, such as the United Kingdom, professional qualifications are usually acquired upon completion of specific professional training that takes place outside and after university. Professional requirements can be set under national law or by professional organisations. Academic recognition and professional recognition are different objectives, and may require different approaches and instruments. However, they do share a methodology for evaluating the educational component of the credential or qualification.

In the context of the international labour market we will concentrate on professional recognition. However, the recognition methodology originated in the framework of academic recognition, so it is important to look briefly at the development of this methodology.

Academic and professional recognition

From the early 1950s to the mid-1970s the purpose of credential evaluation was to establish "equivalence". Diplomas were evaluated on a course-by-course basis and every component of the foreign programme had to be matched with every component in the receiving country's programme. In many countries, in the 1980s the concept of equivalence was replaced by that of recognition: the *recognition* of a diploma, qualification or course of study for a specific purpose. In this sense, recognition means that a qualification which is not completely equivalent is recognised for a certain purpose (for instance entry to a doctoral programme) if it fits that purpose. A foreign degree need not be identical or even almost identical in order to be recognised. It is enough if the foreign degree is of a comparable level and has a comparable function and status, even though it differs in terms of details. So if, for example, a historian has graduated in country A without completing exactly the same number of courses in medieval history as is usual in country B, then he can still be admitted to a Ph.D. course in the host country, as long as the "gap" does not hamper his participation in the Ph.D. programme concerned, assuming that this was the purpose of the evaluation.

Within the concept of recognition, the phenomenon of *acceptance* has gained some ground in Europe in the past decade. Acceptance means that a foreign qualification that is of a slightly *inferior* level, content and/or function to the nearest comparable degree in the receiving country will be accepted at that level if the differences are small enough to be overlooked. Differences might even be highlighted and accepted because of the enrichment that a different educational approach can bring to the host society. The principle is acceptance with respect for the differences. A course from country X which has a lower entrance level than a similar course in country Y might still be accepted, because it is generally similar in content and function. The differences are not disregarded, but accepted. Only when the differences are too substantial is recognition denied.

The Council of Europe/UNESCO (Lisbon) Recognition Convention (1997) adopts the idea of acceptance. The core of this Convention is to emphasise the principle of fair and transparent recognition procedures, and the acknowledgement of differences which should be accepted unless they are found to be substantial. The burden of proof has been laid upon the host country. Transparency regarding the criteria used and procedures followed are the backbone of the Convention. Each party must provide appropriate information on its education system, qualifications and institutions.

Mutual trust in each other's education systems, as a result of growing mobility and increasing information on the different systems, makes such a change of attitude possible. Although some signatory countries specifically underlined that this legal instrument should be seen purely in the framework of academic recognition, the Convention is also very useful for professional recognition. The reason, as pointed out already, is that in principle the methodology in academic recognition is no different from professional recognition *as regards the evaluation of the educational component of the professional qualification*. Of course, what is decisive in the end is the objective of the evaluation: further study or work. In the latter case, the employer might have specific questions for the credential evaluator.

The principle of acceptance is also reflected in the European Union's General Directives for professional recognition (see 2.3).

Transparency instruments

There is another instrument, developed mainly in the field of academic recognition, which is very useful also for professional recognition: the Diploma Supplement. The Diploma Supplement, developed in 1999 by a joint working group of the European Commission, the Council of Europe and UNESCO/CEPES, explains the qualification and the course involved in terms understandable and useful for both academic admissions officers and employers or their HRD departments.

The Diploma Supplement contains the following categories of information:

- information regarding the level of the qualification, the type and status of the awarding institution and the programme followed by the applicant; this information is given in such a way that it does not contain any value judgments or indications regarding possible recognition or "equivalence" in other countries;

- information regarding workload, content and results, together with important additional information, such as the grading scale applied;

- the function of the qualification within the national framework, in terms both of admission to further studies and of the professional status of the holder;

- a short description of the education system of the home country in order to locate the qualification in question within the framework of the national education system of that country.

At this juncture we should also mention the European Credit Transfer System (ECTS), launched in 1989 for the transfer of credits in the framework of regulated student mobility. The main components of the ECTS system are:

- the credit-point system: 60 credits for one academic year;

- the Information Package, a guide for potential partners and students describing courses, curricula, academic and administrative arrangements;

- the Learning Agreement, a contract between student, home institution and host institution describing the courses the student plans to take at the host institution;

- the Transcript of Record, describing the subjects studied, number of credits and grades obtained.

The ECTS is going through a transitional phase, and might ultimately become a credit transfer *and accumulation* system. Although credits might be informative for employers, in our view this tool is mainly useful for academic recognition.

International networks

Last but not least, two very important and active networks are involved in academic recognition. Since the 1980s, the Council of Europe, UNESCO and the Commission of the European Union have been encouraging the development of international networks in the area of academic recognition. EU legislation does not provide any specific regulations governing academic recognition, in contrast to its regulations concerning professional recognition. In 1984 a network of national centres for academic recognition, the National Academic Recognition Information Centres, or NARICs, were established. NARICs meet regularly to exchange information and to discuss any recognition problems that may have arisen and, if possible, solve them.

In 1994 the Council of Europe and CEPES, the higher education department of UNESCO, joined their separate networks to form the European Network of Information Centres on Recognition and Mobility (ENIC). Just as with the NARICs, the most important function of ENIC is to identify recognition problems or issues, and put them on the relevant agendas.

Both networks remain independent. However, given the fact that they are actually staffed by the same national organisations, the NARICs and ENIC collaborate and even have a joint annual meeting. To put it simply, all NARICs are ENICs, but some ENICs – those of countries outside the framework of the European Union, the European Economic Area and the EU Accession Countries – are not members of the NARIC Network. In the past many ENIC and NARIC members have been active in several Council of Europe and UNESCO/CEPES working parties on different issues. Relevant examples include working parties on:

–   transnational education, which resulted in a Code of Good Practice in the Provision of Transnational Education;

–   the methodology of credential evaluation in the light of the Lisbon Recognition Convention, which resulted in the Recommendation on Criteria and Procedures for the Assessment of Foreign Qualifications and Periods of Study;

–   the Russian education system, which resulted in Mutual recognition of qualifications: the Russian Federation and the other European countries;

–   the creation of the international Diploma Supplement;

–   the consequences of the Bologna Process for international recognition, which resulted in the publication of Recognition issues in the Bologna Process – Final report.

Several research projects conducted by the NARIC Network are also relevant:

– accreditation mechanisms in central and eastern Europe;

– recognition of virtual higher education;

– professional recognition: a diversity of methods.

It is important to note that in many countries the NARICs also function as the information point on EU legislation for professional recognition. At their joint annual meeting in Riga in June 2001, both networks also acknowledged the crucial importance of professional recognition as put forward by the Bologna Process.

Professional recognition

The European Union started to tackle professional recognition back in the 1960s and 1970s. The first target was *de jure* professional recognition, which refers to recognition of regulated professions, ranging from physicians and architects to teachers and physiotherapists.

The initial strategy was the harmonisation of the educational curricula of these regulated professions. This resulted in Sectoral Directives, providing for direct recognition. The sectoral directives could be applied only after the majority of the educational programmes leading to a specific professional qualification had been harmonised. However, the growth of the European Union and the fact that harmonisation of education courses was extremely time-consuming forced the policy makers to change strategy. The result was the system of General Directives. The 1989 General Directive for professions requiring tertiary-level education stipulates that qualifications obtained after completion of at least three years of higher education leading to regulated professions in one member state should be recognised in other member states, unless substantial differences can be proved by the competent authorities of the host state.[37] The principle of acceptance, as outlined earlier in this chapter, is reflected in this directive. Coming back to our example of the historian, we might assume that he or she is a secondary school teacher, which is a regulated profession. In the concept of acceptance, differences are in fact welcomed because they have the potential to enrich the profession of history teaching in the receiving country. Less emphasis on medieval history might be compensated for by a greater focus on contemporary history, or on ancient history. However, a possible or even probable gap in knowledge of the national history of the receiving country might be considered too substantial for the qualification to be recognised right away.

---

37. The competent authorities for professional recognition in Europe are either ministries/government-linked agencies or professional organisations.

This was a big leap forward, although the debate as to the precise meaning of the term "substantial differences" will always be a lively one. And if substantial differences are discovered between the qualifications, this might result in non-recognition and under-utilisation of the skills of the professionals involved.

One objection to these procedures is, of course, that they do not tackle the problem of foreigners coming from outside the European Union. There is a trend, in the Netherlands at any rate, towards applying the spirit and methodology of the General Directives to non-EU nationals. But this is certainly not general policy.

The European Union preference for legal solutions is less applicable, however, in the field of *de facto* professional recognition – the recognition of non-regulated professions on the labour market. In this field especially there is a tremendous need for reliable information on the foreign qualification, the educational course leading to it and possible additional requirements. The fact that the labour market is increasingly international only emphasises the urgency of this issue. Governments have to take up this challenge. The national recognition and information centres and their networks are working on it already.

The importance of tackling professional recognition is also visible in the tendency to integrate recognition into trade agreements, by considering education and, therefore, qualifications as *services*. Such initiatives are being undertaken in the framework of the General Agreement on Trade in Services (GATS), and also of regional agreements (NAFTA for North America).

New trends and developments

In the very near future credential evaluators, especially when engaged in professional recognition, will be confronted with an increasing number of applications for the recognition or assessment of qualifications resulting from non-traditional learning. This refers to all sorts of qualifications obtained through learning outside the "regular" classroom. Traditional classroom teaching will give way to other, non-formal, forms of delivery and types of education offered by various educational providers. More and more education will be delivered through the Internet, transnational arrangements and a combination of traditional and non-traditional learning, including work-based learning.

This brings us to the core of the concept of lifelong learning. Through this concept non-traditional learning will be developed for and provided to all generations of students. One major target group is graduate professionals, who need to upgrade, deepen or broaden their competencies in a specific field. The concept of lifelong learning is likely to become an important part of the strategy and mission of higher education. This requires substantial rethinking of the way in which qualifications are earned and recognised. More importantly, it entails a shift of emphasis from education to learning. The focus is shifting from the educational process itself to the output; to the knowledge, skills and attitudes of the graduates; in other words, to their competencies.

In this process the dialogue between higher education institutions, professional organisations and employers will be decisive. These stakeholders will together have to draw up qualifications structures and competencies systems, with government authorities at least monitoring the process. Educational institutions will have to express their learning outcomes in clear and understandable qualifications structures and sets of competencies, which correspond to those used by professional organisations or employers.

The national authorities could go even further than merely monitoring and facilitating the process. They could introduce (and guarantee) the right of citizens, nationals and foreigners to have their competencies assessed at any moment in their professional lives, as indeed some European governments already have. This requires a system of qualifications and competencies recognised on a national scale. Within this system every citizen can ask for an assessment against the background of a certain qualification or set of competencies.

Obviously, in the realm of international recognition, the developments mentioned lead to a focus on the assessment of competencies rather than formal qualifications and the way they have been earned. In order to safeguard the fair recognition of all the possible skills of migrant professionals, it is of the utmost importance to take into account all competencies acquired, regardless of the learning paths.

At the moment, the methodology of traditional credential evaluation is not up to assessing competencies. The criteria used focus on the educational process, such as the entrance level of the course, content and structure, or the rights attached to the qualifications. This process does suffice for formal qualifications, but in the light of the developments and trends foreseen, new forms of assessments will have to be added to the traditional forms of credential evaluation. Accreditation of prior certified or experiential learning – or recognition of informal and non-formal learning, to use another term – is a necessary supplement to traditional credential evaluation for *de facto* recognition. In this way even work-based learning and work experience can be assessed sufficiently.

The ENIC and NARIC Networks have acknowledged this need. At their annual meeting in Riga in 2001, the international networks of recognition information centres therefore proclaimed the development of "other forms of assessment" in addition to traditional credential evaluation or recognition to be one of their top priorities. This has been confirmed at their meetings in Malta (2002) and Vaduz (2003). It is very important that these initiatives are conducted in close co-operation with the other actors in the field: the educational providers, quality assurance agencies, professional organisations, employers and national authorities.

More concretely, projects have been implemented to explore integrating traditional international credential evaluation (ICE) and Prior Learning Assessment and Recognition (PLAR), a term borrowed from Canadian colleagues. Of relevance here is the construction of a NARIC website on ICE and PLAR: http://www.nuffic.nl/ice-plar/.

Conclusion

The globalisation of both the labour market and education, in all its forms, is gathering pace. It is of crucial importance to all parties involved that human resources are used as efficiently as possible in the international context. The traditional methodologies and procedures for assessing qualifications across borders are still indispensable. However, to be able to cope with new trends and developments in the light of lifelong learning, it is necessary to modernise the traditional tools used by credential evaluators for both academic and professional purposes. An intensive dialogue between all relevant actors in the field is vital in the search for successful solutions.

References

Legal framework:

Convention on the Recognition of Qualifications concerning Higher Education in the European Region, Lisbon 1997. Convention of the Council of Europe/UNESCO:
http://conventions.coe.int/treaty/EN/WhatYouWant.asp?NT=165.

The explanatory report to the Convention: http://www.cepes.ro/information_services/sources/on_line/explane.htm.

EU Directives for professional recognition:
http://www.aic.lv/ace/tools/dir_en/default.htm

Codes and standards for credential evaluation:

Recommendation on Criteria and Procedures for the Assessment of Foreign Qualifications, Strasbourg/Bucharest, 2001:
http://www.cepes.ro/hed/recogn/groups/criteria.htm.

The UNESCO-Council of Europe Code of Good Practice in the Provision of Transnational Education, Strasbourg/Bucharest, 2001:
http://www.cepes.ro/hed/recogn/groups/transnat/code.htm.

Recommendation on International Access Qualifications, Strasbourg/ Bucharest, 1999:
http://www.cepes.ro/hed/recogn/groups/recomm.htm

The Bologna Process:

See for an overall website, including all the relevant documents:
http://www.bologna-bergen2005.no

Credential evaluation:

Divis, J. and Scholten, A.M., "Credential Evaluation and Open Distance Learning", in *Virtual Mobility. New technologies and the internationalisation of higher education*, Nuffic Paper 10, 1998, ed. Marijke van der Wende, The Hague, 1998.

Scholten, A.M. & Teuwsen, C.W. (2001) *Widening access to higher education and the labour market: a perspective from the Netherlands*, paper presented at the Glasgow Caledonian University conference on Researching Widening Access. The Hague, 2001.

Scholten, A.M. (2001). *Facilitating mobility of workforce through international recognition of competencies*, paper presented at the second conference on HRD research and practice across Europe, 26-27 January 2001. The Hague, 2001.

Rauhvargers, A., *Qualifications: Instruments and structures for recognition*, paper presented at the Council of Europe Workshop on Lifelong learning for equity and social cohesion: a new challenge to higher education: "Structures and qualifications in lifelong learning", Gozd Martuljek, Krajnska Gora, Slovenia, 9-11 November 2000, Strasbourg, 2000.

The Bologna Process and recognition issues outside the European Higher Education Area

E. Stephen Hunt

Introduction

As I write this contribution, I have the unfair advantage of having read the rapporteur's report and recommendations plus the other papers of the Riga conference. Based on these resources, I propose to address a central theme: why it is important for the emerging EHEA to engage with higher education experts and authorities outside the zone of influence of Bologna, and what it will take to do this.

The United States higher education community is indeed a stakeholder in the Bologna Process, as Timothy Thompson has observed,[38] albeit a stakeholder in a rather peculiar position. The peculiarity arises from the historical fact that those engaged in building the European Higher Education Area (EHEA) have opted to concentrate until very recently on what they call the pan-European dimension of the process despite the reforms themselves having been adopted, in part, to deal with what has loosely been called the "Anglo-Saxon" challenge, a concept that certainly included – and still includes – US higher education. In addition, successive documents, including the Sorbonne Declaration, the Bologna Declaration, the Prague Communiqué and the Berlin Communiqué have all contained statements that one of the goals of the process is to build a more attractive and competitive EHEA and reach out to the world. As a consequence, US higher education has witnessed the Bologna Process from the sidelines even though our system has been cited as both a key incentive and one of the models for the reforms.

The ACA Conference in Hamburg in October 2004 served, at long last, to direct the attention of Bologna reformers to the important question of how these new structures might be viewed outside the EHEA, and recommended that European ministries become active in communicating information outside Europe and engaging external stakeholders in the process.[39] With the Riga Seminar our European colleagues have provided

---

38. Timothy S. Thompson, "The United States as a stakeholder in the Bologna Process," in the present volume.

an opportunity for serious co-operative dialogue to get under way. It goes without saying that this engagement should reach out to all of the world beyond the emerging EHEA. The United States higher education system is a very important non-EHEA system, but so are others.

This chapter will concentrate on four points within the broad theme of engaging with systems outside the EHEA:

1. the fundamental requisites for meaningful mutual dialogue;

2. technical problems in maintaining and increasing US-European recognition and mobility;

3. broader issues of systemic inter-relationship; and

4. recommendations for the next steps to take.

Achieving engagement

Section III of the Lisbon Recognition Convention underscores the fundamental principle that recognition must be mutual, reciprocal, and based on transparent and fair criteria, and the Explanatory Report notes that these principles are intended to operate irrespective of the nature of the education system, the control of institutions within the system, the type of higher education institution, or factors unrelated to recognition per se.[40] The United States and other countries not members of the European Union or the Council of Europe were expressly included in the treaty.[41]

A complex reality

These facts produce several consequences that are relevant to transatlantic educational interaction.

First, while the European Union (EU) and now the emerging EHEA are major actors, the responsibility for recognition matters still falls on the individual member states and states parties, and so there is a dynamic tension between the role of the EU and the emergent EHEA vis-à-vis the role of national authorities. Despite the vision so well described by Stephen Adam, the fact remains that educational authorities remain national, and so even as the EHEA emerges we will continue to deal with individual systems rather than one, and the EHEA will be a kind of super-

---

39. "Recommendations for inclusion in the Bergen Communiqué," ACA Conference on Opening Up to the Wider World? The External Dimension of the Bologna Process, Academic Cooperation Association, Hamburg, 18-19 October 2004.
40. *Convention on the Recognition of Qualifications concerning Higher Education in the European Region*, Lisbon, Portugal, 11 April 1997, Section III, Articles III.1–III.5; and Explanatory Report on the Convention, paragraphs 5, 12, and 23.
41. *Explanatory Report*, ibid., paragraphs 19 and 23.

system rather than a new continental "national" system.[42] Differences in the degree to which individual countries reform their recognition processes or engage in intra- or extra-European dialogue can and do affect post-Bologna interaction. Educators in non-EHEA countries can perhaps be forgiven by our European colleagues if we have difficulty in sorting this out.

Second, the position of non-EHEA countries like the United States is complicated by the degree to which EU or EHEA matters dominate the agenda of the UNESCO European Region, which is quite another entity altogether. There is no doubt that all are conscious of the difference, and that every effort is made to be inclusive and treat the EU and EHEA issues as parallel but separate. However, the importance of the Bologna Process to the European countries within the European Region, and the fact that the European Commission and the Council of Europe are respectively the major underwriter and the co-sponsor of the recognition networks has gradually created a situation in which intra-European issues dominate the agenda. This has the effect of making non-EHEA members of the European Region spectators offering occasional interventions rather than fully engaged partners.

Third, the lack – until recently – of active dialogue and engagement beyond countries bordering the EHEA or seeking entry has led to unintended consequences. EHEA planners and national authorities have been deprived of important information about the higher education systems they seek to benchmark or compete against, such as that of the United States. They have also not had the benefit of early signals as to how other systems would react to specific reforms. The EHEA is a tremendous achievement, and European educational affairs are quite properly a matter for Europeans to manage. But it is rare in history for so complex and thoroughgoing a reform, on such a large scale across so many countries, and in so important a region not to involve input from outside, especially if a key object of the reform is the region's position in the world and other systems are being expressly used as comparison points.

Fourth, proper dialogue and co-operation on recognition issues should concentrate on concerns related to academic quality and the appropriateness of qualifications for the intended use, irrespective of whether the awarding institution is public or private, where it is located, how it delivers education, or if the parent educational system is decentralised. These

---

42. Stephen Adam, "Final report and recommendations of the conference", in the present volume.

important principles have occasionally been lost in the growing controversies over transnational or cross-border education and global trade negotiations. Entire education systems and their philosophies have come under attack, and the fact that we all need to deal with national and international educational scofflaws has been overshadowed by rhetorical, political, and policy issues and actions that range far beyond the actual technical problems that need addressing. The US education system is certainly one of those that has come under this firestorm, and our providers and representatives sometimes feel as if international quality assurance and recognition activities are pursued without regard to, and often deliberately against, the legitimate national interests of our system and our country.

Successes and challenges

To date, the record of US-European engagement on recognition issues appears mixed from a US perspective. A dialogue between European and US higher education experts sponsored by UNESCO-CEPES ended inconclusively in 1994 with the publication of a report in which both sides essentially agreed to disagree on key points.[43] The United States government negotiated and signed the Lisbon Recognition Convention during 1996-1997 and created an ENIC in co-operation with the US higher education associations. From 1997 to 2003 the United States participated actively as an observer in the ENIC Network, but because it remained outside UNESCO and was not a member of the Council of Europe, it could not vote, nor could it help to formulate the ENIC Network work programme. Since 2003 the United States has rejoined UNESCO and thus possesses voting rights, but interaction with European partners has been complicated by the inward focus of dominating Bologna issues and by the emerging issues surrounding transnational education.

During this time, the US ENIC (USNEI) has achieved much success in constructive dialogue on a bilateral and multilateral basis. We have contributed to a better understanding of the US education system and have helped co-ordinate European official engagement with various authorities in the United States. At the same time, we have succeeded in negotiating better treatment of US qualifications and institutional recognition than was the case prior to the Lisbon Convention. Our European colleagues have in the main been forthcoming, frank and co-operative, but there is still a long way to go. For example, there remain numerous situ-

---

43. Stamenka Uvalić-Trumbić, *Guidelines for the Mutual Recognition of Qualifications Between Europe and the United States of America*, Bucharest: UNESCO-CEPES, 1994.

ations within the EHEA where national policies and procedures respecting recognition have not caught up to the spirit or letter of the recognition agreements. The emerging EHEA provides new challenges, because bilateral relations, even where mutually satisfactory, are now beginning to be superseded by laws, policies, and rules that do not always recognise that non-EHEA institutions or their graduates have any status or access. Europeans must work to ensure that the old barriers of national restrictive practices are truly removed, and not just replaced by a pan-European set of barriers defined by the borders of the EU.

Recent problems appear interrelated. For example, the early extra-EHEA focus of the Bologna Process had to do with treating the US higher education system as part of the so-called "Anglo-Saxon challenge." This perspective was connected to the growing phenomenon of exporting educational services beyond national borders and the fact that the United States was one of the leading "exporters" (along with the non-EHEA countries Australia, Canada, and New Zealand, which also belong to the ENIC Network). Russia, also an ENIC member, is another leading "operator", mainly in the countries of the former Soviet Union. And connected to this has been the recent intensive controversy over education services as part of the GATS negotiations, leading to current issues such as the joint UNESCO-OECD project on Guidelines for Quality Assurance in Cross-Border Higher Education.[44] The cumulative result of all these related factors has been to maintain, if not increase, a considerable divide between Europe and the United States with respect to dialogue or co-operation on important recognition issues.

It is time for further openness and co-operation, and for the spirit of the Lisbon Recognition Convention to reanimate the European-US relationship. First, however, there needs to be a basis of mutual understanding based on respect for the systems of higher education on each side. Instead of talking past one another, as in 1994, we must seriously listen, appreciate and work together.

Dismantling myths I – the Anglo-Saxon challenge

A large portion of Guy Haug's section of the *Trends I* paper, presented at the 1999 Bologna Ministerial Conference, was devoted to addressing the observation that:

---

44. See the OECD reports on this project at:
http://www.oecd.org/document/52/0,2340,en_2649_34549_29343796_1_1_1_1,00.html;
and UNESCO's reports at: http://portal.unesco.org/education/en/ev.php-
URL_ID=29228&URL_DO=DO_TOPIC&URL_SECTION=201.html.

"Among the fears heard in the debate about the value of a 3-5-8 model was the possibility that Europe might just import a foreign, 'Anglo-Saxon' (and mainly American) model".[45]

Clearly, the Bologna exercise was viewed from the beginning – at least by political leaders – as a pre-emptive reply to a putative challenge posed by the so-called global "Anglo-Saxon" or "American" model. This perspective – however flawed – remains important in the EHEA, as was indicated as recently as the OECD/Norway Forum on Trade in Education Services in 2003.[46]

The notion that there is a single Anglo-Saxon model or degree structure is novel, certainly to so-called Anglo-Saxons! It is also quite incorrect. The British or UK degree "system" is, as most know, actually three different systems. The US higher education philosophy and degree system is derived as much or more from Scottish (undergraduate) and German (graduate) traditions as English, despite the prevailing shibboleth that our education system is a derivation of English institutions.[47]

There are manifold differences among the nearly 90 national education systems that have evolved, or adopted, some or most of the characteristics that define the "Anglo-Saxon" model: bachelor-master-doctor degree systems, undergraduate education emphasising breadth as well as depth, maximum flexibility in study programmes, transferable credit, complex admissions systems permitting various routes of access, institutional self-financing, employer partnerships, and interinstitutional competition. The origins of these ideas may have been influenced by concepts current in Europe and parts of the British Isles between the revolt of Martin Luther and the Thirty Years' War, but they have spread and transformed across the intervening half-millennium and are now mature systems in their own right.

These systems are equally the product of indigenous needs and contributions as well as diverse Western and non-Western traditions. None of these education systems, whether in London, Edinburgh, New York, Toronto, Quebec, Cape Town, Mumbai, Tokyo, Dublin, Manila, Woomera, Beijing or elsewhere is or would particularly wish to be labelled as "Anglo-Saxon". Furthermore, a few of them are even inside the European Union

45. Guy Haug and Jette Kirstein, *Trends in Learning Structures in Higher Education (I)*, 7 June 1999, Confederation of European Union Rectors' Conferences and the Association of European Universities (CRE), pp. 7-8.
46. Marijk van der Wende and Robin Middlehurst, *Cross-Border Postsecondary Education in Europe*, Paris: OECD/CERI and Trondheim, Norway, November 3-4, 2003, p. 15.
47. See Douglas Sloan, *The Scottish Enlightenment and the American College Ideal*, New York: Teachers College Press, 1971; and Richard J. Storr, *The Beginnings of Graduate Education in America*, Chicago: University of Chicago Press, 1953.

and not in external competition with it. And several, including that of the United States, are inside the European Region and purportedly the partners and not the nemesis of Europe!

As to the idea of challenge or competition, this is simply a fact of higher education in the modern world, regardless of country. Van der Wende and Middlehurst provided ample evidence in their Trondheim presentation of the efforts of European countries to export education services and to attract international students.[48] Indeed, they pointed out that the *Trends III* report cited the attractiveness of the EHEA – an elegant euphemism for competition – as the third most important goal of the EHEA countries.[49] Competition for students, resources, and prestige is not an "Anglo-Saxon" plot or a perversion introduced into higher education by the United States. It is a necessity that has inevitably evolved as the consequence of needing to serve more and more students with finite resources, economic and social development, and the pursuit of individual and institutional aims. Dialogue and engagement outside the EHEA will not prove very fruitful if the EHEA is seen to be hypocritical on the issue of competition and its shadow twin, protectionism.

Dismantling myths II – US education as a world problem

It is true that aspects of the US system can sometimes be strange to those used to traditional European organisation and structure. For example, the US system is characterised by aggressive competition for funding, students, faculty, and research opportunities among its institutions. The historical facts of undeveloped frontiers, missionary activity, the blending of indigenous and immigrant practices, and the lack of pre-existing governmental systems supporting institutional higher education meant that private organisations founded many higher education establishments. It also meant that even state institutions were expected from an early date to supplement meagre public funding with independent earnings, including student fees. Furthermore, the US institutions themselves had to be established as free corporations due to the lack of other oversight bodies, and self-governance even extended to joint quality assurance mechanisms independent of the state.

The tendency of the US higher education system to offer flexibility is also noteworthy. Access to higher education, for example, is based on case-by-case assessment of individual student records, test scores, and other evidence rather than by provisions enshrined in national framework

---

48. Van der Wende and Middlehurst, pp. 8-16.
49. Ibid., p. 15.

laws and applied universally. The prevailing philosophy is that appropriate accommodation should be made for all students showing potential, and multiple access points are available. Likewise, study programmes are structured with attention given to breadth as well as depth, interdisciplinary study is favoured, and transferring is made possible both horizontally (between programmes and institutions) as well as vertically for talented students who can move up faster than others. Flexibility may have originated in the early nineteenth century when the United States was a developing nation, but its real dominance dates to the rise of educational and research collaboration between institutions and employers.

The education system prevailing throughout the United States and associated territories is now several centuries old and is as authentically national as anything in Europe. Features originally necessitated by circumstance have evolved into sophisticated modern legal and organisational practices. (Harvard, the oldest US university, is older than all but 70 existing European universities, being barely younger than Utrecht and Budapest but older than Bamberg, Göttingen, Moscow, Oslo and many others. Four universities in the Western hemisphere are even older than Harvard.)

US higher education has its problems, not least of which are the trade-offs inherent in so decentralised a system. Reliance on self-policing to assure quality is one feature that not a few outside authorities have criticised, especially as this is perceived as contributing to inconsistent standards and the phenomenon of diploma mills. There is not space in this paper to give full justice to this issue, but two points are relevant to the present discussion.

One is the fact that how something so complex and nationally authentic as an education system has evolved, and its basic characteristics, are not things that can or should be regarded as recognition barriers. Education systems as diverse as that of the Philippines, where access to university occurs after the tenth year of school; the former Soviet system, where structure and ideology were intimately intertwined; traditional two-tier European systems based on highly selective and advanced secondary-level access; and that of the US have coexisted and interrelated without insurmountable problems caused by systemic differences. It is difficult to see why, all of a sudden, the nature of the US system's organisation and structure should be a major obstacle in discussions of mutual recognition and quality assurance.

The other point to consider is that a good argument can be made that the rise of scofflaws in the world of education has more to do with the rigidity and unpreparedness of hosts and exporters than it does with the basic organisational theory of education systems. Frauds and substandard providers come into being because no one can stop them, no one chooses to stop them, or no one is alerted to their existence. Since we still exist in a world of national competent authorities, national authorities must be enabled to combat fraud. Stephen Adam would recommend that national framework laws be created to assure quality.[50] However, care needs to be exercised to ensure that EHEA frameworks do not simply replace one set of failed templates with another. The universal tendency of officialdom (our agencies are guilty of this, too) is to rely on the letter of regulatory guidance rather than its spirit or the discretion permitted. Without reform of procedures and organisational cultures as well as frameworks, the latter could devolve into opaque barriers rather than transparent facilitators (no framework law means no, or limited, recognition).

Framework laws at national level are not a possible or practical solution in many non-EHEA countries, including the United States. Are we then to be suspected of poor standards or failure to combat fraud because our Constitution forbids an EHEA-style response? This would be a most unfortunate situation. In fact, the US higher education community and governments at all federal levels have been attacking fraud for many years, and getting better at it. To cite only a few examples, the US Congress has recently instructed federal agencies to get tougher on diploma mills; several states have followed or are following Oregon in instituting laws tightening accreditation requirements for licensing providers; and our recognised accreditation agencies are actively pursuing ways to improve standards, both for domestically accredited campuses and those abroad. [51] Fraud operators, recognising that operating openly in the United States is getting more difficult, are now moving overseas. Much activity of this kind is now located in less-developed countries where the national education systems do not have the capacity, the tradition of independent legal authority or civic culture, or the contacts with international information networks to avoid becoming victims.

---

50. Stephen Adam, "The impact of emerging qualifications frameworks on recognition," in the present volume.
51. See Robert J. Cramer, Office of Special Investigations, "Diploma mills are easily created and some have issued degrees to federal employees at government expense", testimony before the Senate Subcommittee on 21st Century Competitiveness, Washington: GAO Report 04-1096T, September 23, 2004; US Office of Personnel Management, *Qualifications Standards Manual*, General Policies and Instructions, Part E.4-E.4(a), February 3, 2005; Council on Higher Education Accreditation (CHEA), International Quality Review website, http://www.chea.org/International/index.asp; and the Oregon Office of Degree Authorization home page at http://www.osac.state.or.us/oda/.

Unless there is an international effort to share information among national authorities and build capacity in many countries, the efforts of the EHEA, the United States, and other developed systems to stop fraud will have the unintended consequence of exporting it elsewhere.

Dismantling myths III – European education as a US problem

American educators are equally guilty of harbouring misunderstandings and prejudices concerning European education and current reform efforts. While many US educational authorities and experts are familiar with European education systems and even with Bologna, the actual number is quite small when one considers the size and scope of US higher education. As with Europe, the United States has tended to be focused on its internal issues and reforms to the exclusion of conscious, deliberate, and genuinely inclusive outside engagement. The outcome of the 1994 CEPES dialogue, as well as some historical decisions regarding US credential evaluation, have shown that Americans can be as uninformed and mistake-prone as their European counterparts.

Americans do tend to believe that European education systems are characterised by complexity, institutionalised stratification, academic inflexibility, administrative inflexibility, and attitudes towards non-European education systems ranging from ignorance and contempt to uncertainty and protectionism. Many are the stories of US graduates and educators who have encountered bewildering definitions of "higher education;" impossible barriers to access – even for outstanding candidates – raised by the "equivalence" bureaucracies and rules of various national governments and commissions; discovered that qualifying for a state-subsidised scholarship or a research grant is often easier than gaining recognition for qualifications or access to higher education or work; or found that knowledge of non-European education systems varies greatly and often has depended upon the interests of the personalities in charge (or their prejudices) and whether the non-European country had at one time been a colony or an enemy. While these impressions are based on true events, it is important for US educators to realise that comparable tales of woe, based on equally factual instances, could be related by Europeans about their encounters with US education.

Because the US system is not centrally regulated, because access is distinguished from outcomes in US notions of quality, and because European regulatory systems tended to ignore non-state and non-national education, American institutions often sought informal relationships with European partners or established outposts that did not require the intervention of national authorities and often could not have met local requirements for national recognition. Since these arrangements did not seek to become part of the national (read: state) systems, and were private, they were largely ignored. This all changed from the late 1980s onwards because of the beginning of European moves towards what would become the Bologna Process and the parallel changes and improvements in international recognition and quality assurance. Another important development was the tremendous increase in international demand for US-style programmes such as bachelor's and master's degrees, together with high demand for programmes offered by UK, Australian, Canadian, and New Zealand institutions. (This factor, coupled with the collapse of the Soviet Union and the adoption of three-cycle degree systems in many European countries, marks the probable genesis of the notion of an "Anglo-Saxon" challenge.) Coming on the heels of these changes was the Internet and the explosion of new educational opportunities and novel means to deliver them. History was moving at a pace faster than traditional authorities were prepared for.

The cumulative effects of all these events, interactions, and phenomena have been to reinforce mutual stereotypes and limit interaction. Some American educators and educational leaders, particularly those actively engaged in international education and programmes outside the United States, see the EHEA and the evolving international work on quality assurance as raising new challenges rather than opportunities, particularly to long-established inter-institutional ties and to the mutual recognition of qualifications. They are not well enough informed about EHEA, and neither side has explained its jargon or its aims to the other in clear terms. Americans know, as Robin Middlehurst and Steve Woolfield have pointed out, that the world of higher education has permanently changed and that global mobility and interchange is a reality.[52] The legitimate US transnational providers and partners in traditional programmes are frequently right to insist that some of the current recognition and quality assurance issues are caused by outmoded approaches and unfair practices in host countries. But American educators need to know more about the problems that are not due to the hosts but rather to exporters' behaviour. The way to overcome these problems and resolve issues is to first realise that each side has legitimate interests and legitimate traditions, and then be willing to examine one's own practices in order to reach a mutually satisfactory result. If Americans insist, as we must, that our counterparts

---

52. Robin Middlehurst and Steve Woolfield, "The role of transnational, private and for-profit provision in meeting global demand for tertiary eucation: mapping, regulation, and impact", Summary Report to the Commonwealth of Learning and UNESCO, Vancouver, CA: COL, October 2003.

recognise our legitimacy and work with our system, so we must recognise and work with theirs.

A renewed opportunity

In the background paper for the Bologna ministerial conference, Guy Haug and Jette Kirstein concisely identified the internal European issues requiring attention:

–   [The] type, breadth and duration of secondary education, with obvious consequences concerning age and preparation for further studies;

–   the existence or not of sub-systems of higher education, their respective role and size and the relationship between them, in particular possibilities to transfer from one to the other;

–   access to higher education (from open choice to various forms of selection – a *numerus clausus* in all or some sectors);

–   study fees (from gratuity to differential or generalised systems of tuition fee);

–   organisation of studies in terms of calendar (from annual courses to block modules), choice (varying from set curricula to nearly free choice), frequency and type of examinations (continuous examinations, final exams per credit, or only block examination after several semesters of study);

–   and of course, the structure, duration, number and type of degrees that can be earned.[53]

What is intriguing about these issues is that they go a long way towards defining a higher education system that is close enough to North American practice to reward a technical dialogue concerning details. These six points, if put another way, aim at a system that:

–   is actively concerned about the social and economic relevance of education;

–   recognises that modern higher education must serve diverse populations with varying types of preparation, and provide access for them in appropriate ways;

–   recognises the essential multidisciplinarity of academic and professional life, as well as the interplay between theory and application, and encourages flexibility as well as providing transfer opportunities;

53. *Trends I*, ibid., p. 5.

- realises that general or broad education does not cease with secondary school, but continues throughout life and must be reflected in
  formal curricula as part of building towards a coherent subject concentration;

- understands that the costs of higher education cannot be borne by the
  state alone, but must be shared by all beneficiaries of such education,
  corporate and individual; and

- responds to these challenges by designing and offering a wide variety of study options organised into a few well-recognised qualifications and levels that form a progressive system.

The US higher education system is conceived along similar structural and
institutional lines. EHEA institutions and academic structures may not
reach the degree of decentralisation and institutionalised flexibility char-
acteristic of the United States, but that is not necessary. What has been
achieved by the implementation of the Bologna Process is the start of
reorganisation along modern international lines. The EHEA system will
permit much greater programmatic and transfer flexibility; it will use a
few universally understood indicators of attainment (degrees, Diploma
Supplement, ECTS credits); and it will begin to institute articulation
between post-secondary vocational/technical education and access to
appropriate higher education. US educators can also hope that the acceptance of the need for cross-disciplinary breadth and post-secondary general education, demanded by employers, will enable European educators
to begin to understand why these are so important in US higher education
and why they have made our "brand" of higher education so sought after
and successful.

Technical issues needing attention

Credit calculation

The *Tuning* report has pointed out that credits "are just a system to
express the equivalence (volume) of learning," and that ECTS credits
"are calculated from the base position of 60 credits being equivalent to
one average European full-time year of learning."[54] The report also
observes that an academic year lasting 12 months might result in an
award of up to 75 credits, counting summer and inter-term sessions.[55]
ECTS credits also measure only what was done within the parameters for

---

54. Julia González and Robert Wagenaar, *Tuning Educational Structures In Europe*,
Report to the European Commission, Brussels, 31 May 2002, pp. 106 and 109.
55. Ibid., p. 106.

awarding the credit, and not necessarily how well it was done in terms of standard or grade.[56] And, since ECTS credits are tied to the specific subject curriculum, this means that they may not always mean the same thing because European post-secondary education frequently differentiates between such things as university and non-university studies and assigns different sublevels to even similar subjects taught in different academic venues.[57]

The purposes outlined for ECTS resemble those for US credit hours to some degree, as do the components used to calculate how much credit to assign for a module (or course, in US parlance) based on expected student workload.[58] However, there are differences that experts on each side need to address. It would be particularly helpful for US educators to understand how the content and calculation of ECTS credits varies according to the nature of the programme, where it is taught, and what the subject is considered to represent.

What is more problematic is the definition of an academic year in terms of credits. The accepted US procedure operates on the assumption that most variations in the full-time academic year are not significant if the level and type of education is comparable.[59] Higher education at degree level is based almost universally on one of the historic European university models, with academic year calendars that typically involve two semesters or terms, or three out of four quarters. Summer sessions and inter-term periods are added in only if they have actually been attempted and credits earned. International credit calculations in the United States start with a record of the number of foreign credits accumulated in an academic year (or term or other comparable time period) as calculated in the home system or institution; divide this total by the number of US credit hours that would be earned in full-time study during the same period, and use the quotient as the divisor for determining the number of US credit hours additional foreign credits represent.[60]

In a standard full-time US academic year, 30 credit hours is the typical amount earned. If 60 ECTS credits are awarded for the same period and represent a comparable workload, which they do, then the resulting divisor would be 2, and the ECTS credits would be divided by half to approximate the comparable number of US credit hours. The formula would

56. Ibid., p. 116.
57. Ibid., p. 116
58. Ibid., p. 124.
59. Joseph Sevigny, co-ordinator, *The AACRAO International Guide: A Resource for International Education Professionals*, Washington: AACRAO, 2001, Chapter 8, p. 71.
60. Ibid., p. 73.

naturally be adjusted for different academic calendars and different types of credit. It would be useful for US and European experts to have a serious technical discussion about the comparability of credits, and to also refer to comparative calculations of other credit systems such as UMAP (University Mobility Asia-Pacific).

Degree structures

The problems with comparing credits lead logically to the issue of what constitutes an academic or professional degree at a given level. The Helsinki Conference and Salamanca Convention have apparently set the Bologna bachelor's degrees as ranging from 180-240 ECTS credits.[61] US bachelor's degrees are required by accreditation guidelines and institutional policy to be at least 120 US credit hours (semester system) or more, and this is confirmed in federal law in order for students to be defined as full-time for purposes of eligibility for student assistance. Obviously, under the current formula this would potentially mean that only EHEA bachelor's programmes with ECTS credits totalling 240 could be considered comparable unless additional factors were considered. Since the bachelor's degree gives access to all subsequent programmes in both systems, a technical discussion of this issue would be advisable.

One good result of the EHEA move to acceptance of credit for measuring workload at all degree levels is that this may end confusion over the US practice of assigning academic credit for all academic work, including independent research. In the past, some European authorities questioned US master's and doctoral degrees because credit hours were awarded for theses and dissertations, leading some to wonder if this work represented research studies of a standard comparable to European degrees. What US institutions were doing is exactly what is now required under the adoption of the ECTS by the Bologna Process, namely using credit to record academic work of a variety of types. In order to maintain full-time registration (enrolment) as a student, even research degree candidates are awarded modules of credits for designing and conducting research and writing major papers. If and when the ECTS is expanded to include advanced degree programmes, Europeans will be doing the same thing. This same point has been made another way by Volker Gehmlich in his study of the variety of uses to which ECTS credits might be put.[62] Gehmlich also notes, quite rightly, that the use of credit – like other quality

---

61. *Tuning* Report, pp. 110 and 117.
62. Volker Gehmlich, "Recognition of Credits – Achievements and Challenges", in the present volume.

assurance mechanisms – is dependent for success on the integrity of those employing it as well as a good understanding of what it means.

A more serious issue is that the 3-2 degree structure chosen for the Bologna Process may have been derived from a misunderstanding of so-called "Anglo-Saxon" degree structures. Guy Haug made a statement towards the end of the *Trends I* paper, while discussing the earlier Sorbonne Declaration, which is interesting:

> "The annexes to the report [the Attali report for the French Government] pro-vide a rather short introduction to a few foreign systems, with surprising asser-tions such as the alleged similarity between French IUTs on the one hand, and German Fachhochschulen and former British polytechnics on the other. In the case of the UK, four-year honours and Scottish degrees are not mentioned, and the role of sub-degree diplomas is ignored. The presentation of the US system mentions four-year bachelor's and the great many community colleges offer-ing two-year qualifications, but these facts seem not to have been taken into account in the recommendations. The report does not actually attempt to jus-tify its reference to a would-be European pattern of qualifications in two stages (a first degree/qualification after three years, followed by post-degrees studies leading either to a master's after altogether five years or a doctorate after altogether eight years). It seems to be based mainly on the awareness of trends and reforms announced or in progress in the UK, Italy and Germany at the time with a perceived convergence on a first degree after three years."[63]

A related degree-definition issue is the nature of the bachelor's degree programme, notwithstanding length or number of credits. Many, but not all, European national authorities and higher education institutions still refuse to recognise a US bachelor's degree as representing tertiary work. It is usually claimed that the first two years of study, during which time most US students study a programme of distributed requirements cover-ing several subjects, comprise secondary-level studies. The stated reasons for this non-recognition include the inferior standard of US secondary diplomas, incompatibility with national requirements that students study only a single subject, and unclear regulations as to how these credits are earned and why. Such policies also apparently explain why the US asso-ciate degree is even more rarely recognised and why the US degree system is described as similar to the Bologna system – the third degree is simply ignored. The issue is further complicated by a tendency to state the non-recognition in a manner implying a summary judgment on the whole system.

---

63. Guy Haug, "The Sorbonne Declaration of 25 May 1998: what it does say, what it doesn't", in *Trends I*, ibid., p. 57.

There is no doubt that European secondary school-leaving standards often exceed the requirements stated for US high school diplomas. But US students are not admitted to most US higher education institutions on the basis of school-leaving requirements alone. Instead, they are assessed on the basis of additional academic and personal achievement. These requirements stipulate not only high school work at the top end of the range of standards represented by that generic diploma, but also scores in tests (including the Advanced Placement examinations used to screen US students by European institutions), essays, oral interviews, and other evidence. Once enrolled, so-called distribution requirements are set in conference with a student's faculty advisor and tailored to supplement the subject concentration. None of this is secondary work, and US accreditation rules forbid the award of credit for work not at tertiary standard, such as remedial studies. Furthermore, the first degrees of national systems that recognise US bachelor's degrees, such as Australia, China, Japan, Canada, and the UK, are accepted in Europe, while ours often are not. This situation is neither logically defensible nor acceptable, and the issue is one that needs to be resolved so that it does not colour progress in other recognition areas.

Broader issues

US-European interchange

It is logical that EHEA higher education institutions and the EU seek to improve the mobility of students within EHEA and wish to concentrate primarily on attracting more intra-European traffic, as was reported in the *Trends III* report.[64] There are, however, historic, economic, and policy reasons for wanting to maintain, and if possible increase, the transatlantic flow of academic talent. The EHEA and North America remain two of the world's chief sources of intellectual vigour and productivity, and they are among each other's main trade and research partners. Hundreds of EHEA and US academic and professional institutions maintain active partnerships for research and the exchange of students and faculty. And, while the numbers of student flows in both directions are smaller than each system's flows with other world regions, there is continued active interest on both sides for more opportunities. These flows can be made easier if each side is more engaged on mutual recognition issues, and the current effort to reach out beyond EHEA is a good example.

---

64. Sybille Reichert and Christian Tauch, *Trends 2003: Progress toward the European Higher Education Area – steps toward sustainable reform of higher education in Europe*, Brussels: European University Association and European Commission, July 2003, pp. 34-38.

Security concerns have without doubt affected student flows to the United States, but this situation is not as dire, nor as isolated to the United States situation, as some reports have indicated. Since the implementation of new US visa and immigration measures beginning in late 2001, the overall flow of students to the United States began to show a slight decline only last academic year (2003-2004). Efforts are already under way to resolve most of the major problems, including delays in obtaining visas and fees. The declines themselves have been unevenly distributed across different countries, and evidence suggests that other host countries experienced similar hiccoughs in international student flows during the same period.[65] US student flows to study overseas, primarily to Europe, have continued to show annual gains.[66]

Trade and GATS issues

Trade issues are within the competence of authorised negotiating parties, such as sovereign governments and, for the Member States, the EU. In this respect, it is possible that recognition questions could arise in the sphere of mobility of professional persons, since in many countries the recognition of professional licenses also involves the recognition of qualifications upon which the license may be based. However, this matter is currently outside the work programme of the ENIC Network because it has to do with high-level economic and trade policy as well as issues, such as licensing and work visas, that lie outside the competent jurisdiction of education authorities. Jindra Divis has proposed a number of ideas in his seminar paper that are interesting.[67] Most cases of recognition of professional qualifications and licences, however, do not use the new principles of recognition but are based on detailed proof of "equivalence" that is in turn governed by laws and policies regarding labour markets and national economic policies. It is unlikely that educational recognition experts in most countries would take up these matters without adherence to these standards and with authorisation to do so.

Trade issues have entered the recognition arena due to the broader issue of transnational or cross-border education. It is important, in this author's view, that the questions of recognition and quality assurance with respect to transnational education be the focus of discussion, not the questions of

---

65. The British Council, for example, reported that East Asian, and specifically Chinese, visas were expected to decline in 2004-2005 due to increased security requirements and travel concerns. See CEMIS Market Report, April-May 2004.
66. Hey-Kyung Koh Chin, ed., *Open Doors 2004: Report on International Educational Exchange*, New York: Institute of International Education, November 2004.
67. Jindra Divis, "Recognition for the labour market", in the present volume.

higher trade policy which lie outside the education field. The best service that recognition professionals can bring to the debates on transnational provision of education is to promote the serious study of the factors that should define what a recognisable traditional or non-traditional educational programme or qualification should possess, and also its provider. This focus should include the reform of recognition practices and procedures to permit non-traditional programmes to be addressed and given due consideration; suggestions for what is needed in home and host systems in order to deal with transnational providers and make appropriate decisions; and expanded intra- and interregional information sharing among competent authorities.

Next steps

Bologna is a systemic educational reform that is pan-European. The scale and set of goals represented by Bologna are breathtaking, as is the pace of reform set by the goal of establishing the new framework by 2010. Since reaching out beyond the EHEA is a central goal of the Bologna Process, opening up the Bologna dialogue to non-EHEA countries has the potential to alleviate the awkward status of spectator that has been the lot of ENICs located outside the EHEA. It would also help to fulfil the main purpose of the recognition conventions, which is to improve information sharing and mutual co-operation within and across regions as a way to foster mobility.

Among the steps that could be considered at this stage are the following:

– Recommend that EHEA higher education institutions with US and other non-EHEA partner institutions inform their partners about Bologna degree developments and actively seek to work out any issues in order to preserve fruitful co-operation and establish precedents that can be used to inform recognition policies.

– Renew the dialogue between US educators, including but not limited to the National Council on the Evaluation of Foreign Educational Credentials, which was terminated in 1994. USNEI would also be part of this process.

– Make every effort to bring EHEA and non-EHEA experts and leaders together, both in the North American context and other interregional contexts, to expand understanding of their education systems. North American/EHEA interaction could involve Canadian as well as US educators.

– Ensure that the current effort to focus EHEA on the world outside its borders is reflected in how the work programmes of the ENIC and

NARIC Networks evolve, and consider entering into formal interregional arrangements and co-operation.

- Maintain and support workable and affordable solutions to cross-system issues like information sharing, such as the highly successful ENIC-NARIC Web portal.

- Work together to address timely concerns that are shared by EHEA and non-EHEA systems alike such as: (1) promotion of better international co-operation in quality assurance; (2) developing new and workable solutions to quality assurance and recognition of non-traditional education; (3) ensuring that the EHEA stays open to cross-border provision of education, partnerships, and mobility from outside; (4) resolving recognition and mobility issues that arise when systems are organised and structured differently from the EHEA; and (5) continuing to deal with academic and professional scofflaws and frauds.

In accomplishing these steps or any others that may be chosen, it will be good for all to bear in mind these fundamentals of the process:

- Recognise that reforms and changes have not obviated the need for recognition and quality assurance professionals, but have in fact increased the complexity and scope of their work, and plan training exercises and professional seminars to reflect this fact. US experts could participate as appropriate.

- Endeavour, on both sides, to show increased respect for how systems legitimately differ so that work can focus on the technical issues and realistic solutions, and not become sidetracked by tangential issues or fall prey to untested assumptions. (This would apply, of course, to bilateral engagement with any country or region.)

- Be willing to change what is mistaken, impractical, or illogical but recognise that this will not happen overnight, since recognition processes are often governed by rules, procedures and bodies outside the control of the recognition community, and other interests have a stake in the resolution of educational issues.

- Recognition and mobility must derive, ultimately, from an acceptance of one another's cultural realities and authentic national systems.

US educators have maintained close ties to European institutions and faculties since the colonial era. While proud of their own educational system, they are also aware of its shortcomings and are constantly engaged in reform debates and processes. They have a great respect for the European system, and would welcome the opportunity to participate as appropriate in the refinement of the Bologna reforms from an external standpoint. There is also a mutual need to maintain and strengthen existing academic ties and ensure that policies developed on either side do not inadvertently harm long-standing relationships.

Working together is different now from in the past, for neither the US nor the EHEA is the primary source, or destination, of academic talent for the other. New and important educational leaders have emerged in Asia, Latin America, Africa, and Oceania. They are rapidly becoming attractive competitors in the global academic marketplace themselves. Neither we nor they should look upon this marketplace as a commercial marketplace, for the English word "market" does not automatically connote business, but rather exchange and interaction. Higher education inevitably imports many aspects of corporate behaviour as it becomes more independent of the state, more accountable, and serves a wider variety of both stakeholders and students. Some higher education will be, and is, offered by for-profit entities. But the professional question before us is not to confuse organisation, management, and operation with the essence of education. These are means, not ends. Rather, our collective purpose is to develop and implement strategies and mechanisms for promoting mobility while helping to assure quality academic and professional experiences. Together, we can.

Sources

Adam, Stephen. Final report and recommendations of the conference in the present volume.

Adam, Stephen. "The impact of emerging qualifications frameworks on recognition," in the present volume.

Convention on the Recognition of Qualifications concerning Higher Education in the European Region, Lisbon, Portugal, 11 April 1997.

Cramer, Robert J. Office of Special Investigations, "Diploma mills are easily created and some have issued degrees to federal employees at government expense", Testimony before the Senate Subcommittee on 21st Century Competitiveness, Washington: GAO Report 04-1096T, 23 September 2004.

Divis, Jindra. "Recognition for the labour market", in the present volume.

Explanatory Report to the Convention on the Recognition of Qualifications concerning Higher Education in the European Region, Lisbon, Portugal, 11 April 1997.

Gehmlich, Volker. "Recognition of credits – Achievements and challenges", in the present volume.

González, Julia and Robert Wagenaar, *Tuning educational structures in Europe*, Report to the European Commission, Brussels, 31 May 2002.

Haug, Guy and Jette Kirstein. *Trends in learning structures in higher education (I)*, 7 June 1999, Confederation of European Union Rectors' Conferences and the Association of European Universities (CRE).

Koh Chin, Hey-Kyung, ed. *Open Doors 2004: report on international educational exchange*, New York: Institute of International Education, November 2004.

Middlehurst, Robin and Steve Woolfield. *The role of transnational, private and for-profit provision in meeting global demand for tertiary education: mapping, regulation, and impact*, Summary Report to the Commonwealth of Learning and UNESCO, Vancouver, CA: COL, October 2003.

"Recommendations for Inclusion in the Bergen Communiqué," ACA Conference on Opening up to the wider world? The external dimension of the Bologna Process, Academic Cooperation Association, Hamburg, 18-19 October 2004.

Reichert, Sybille and Christian Tauch, *Trends 2003: Progress toward the European Higher Education Area – Steps toward sustainable reform of higher education in Europe*, Brussels: European University Association and European Commission, July 2003.

Sevigny, Joseph, co-ordinator, *The AACRAO international guide: a resource for international education professionals*, Washington: AACRAO, 2001.

Sloan, Douglas. *The Scottish Enlightenment and the American college ideal*, New York: Teachers College Press, 1971.

Storr, Richard J. *The beginnings of graduate education in America*, Chicago: University of Chicago Press, 1953.

Thompson, Timothy S. "The United States as a stakeholder in the Bologna Process", in the present volume.

US Office of Personnel Management, *Qualifications Standards Manual*, General Policies and Instructions, Part E.4-E.4(a), February 3, 2005.

Uvalic-Trumbic, Stamenka. *Guidelines for the mutual recognition of qualifications between Europe and the United States of America*, Bucharest: UNESCO-CEPES, 1994.

Van der Wende, Marijk, and Robin Middlehurst. *Cross-border post-secondary education in Europe*, Paris: OECD/CERI and Trondheim, Norway, 3-4 November 2003.

Programmes, providers and accreditors on the move: implications for the recognition of qualifications

Jane Knight

Introduction

Focus on the mobility of programmes and providers

Two key goals of the Bologna Process are to increase the attractiveness of the European Higher Education Area to the rest of the world and to promote greater academic mobility within and outside Europe. Both aspects require that attention be given to the importance of recognising qualifications across borders. When discussing the implications of recognising credentials across borders one automatically thinks about people – students, new graduates or professionals – moving to another country in order to pursue further studies or to undertake new employment opportunities. The mobility of both students and professionals raises important considerations for the process of ensuring that their academic and professional qualifications are recognised in jurisdictions other than where the award or professional designation was obtained. In the past decade, increased attention has been given to this issue, but at the same time, another element of cross-border education has surfaced which requires further attention and that is the movement of academic programmes and institutions/providers across borders.

Increased demand for higher education

There is ample evidence that demand for higher education in the next twenty years will outstrip the capacity of some countries to meet the domestic need. Furthermore, there is growing interest in "international higher education" as a way to gain an internationally recognised qualification for future study and work in other countries. *The Global Student Mobility 2025 Report* (2002) prepared by IDP Education Australia predicts that the demand for international education will increase from 1.8 million international students in 2000 to 7.2 million international students in 2025.

By all accounts these are staggering figures and present enormous challenges and opportunities. Students moving to other countries to pursue their studies will remain an important part of the international dimension of higher education. But student mobility will not be able to satisfy the enormous appetite for higher education from densely populated countries wanting to build human capacity or from students wanting an internationally recognised award. Hence the emergence and growing importance of transnational/cross-border education programmes and providers. It is not known what proportion of the demand will be met by student mobility, but it is clear that there will be exponential growth in the movement of programmes and institutions/providers across national borders. New types of providers, new forms of delivery and new models of collaboration are being developed in order to take education programmes to students in their home countries.

The purpose of this paper is to focus attention on the challenges and questions relating to the "recognition" of the qualifications from the delivery of education courses and programmes across national/regional boundaries. More attention is given to mobility in and out of the European Higher Education Area, than within Europe per se. The emphasis is clearly placed on education programmes and providers crossing national jurisdictional borders – not only the students. There are enormous implications for national education regulatory and policy frameworks for both sending and receiving countries resulting from cross-border education. It also involves complementary regional/international regulatory and normative initiatives.

Terminology

The vocabulary of quality assurance, accreditation and recognition can aptly be described as either a maze or minefield. Each country uses these concepts in ways that make sense in terms of its regulatory, policy, cultural and linguistic environment. It is thus very easy to get confused and lost in the maze of different approaches or accidentally trip up in interpreting a concept in a different way from that intended. For the purposes of this discussion, quality recognition and assurance is used in a general sense and includes quality audit, evaluation, accreditation and other review processes and elements.

The language of internationalisation is also changing and differs between countries and regions. The terms used to describe the movement of education across borders are a good example. The term education providers is now becoming a more common and inclusive term as it includes both the more traditional higher education institutions as well as the organisations, networks, governments and companies all of whom are providing tertiary education. This paper uses the term providers to mean all types of entities that are offering education programmes and services. There is some criticism directed towards the use of the term "providers" as it seems to be buying into the "marketisation and corporatisation" agenda. This is a sign of the times and indeed, every attempt is made in this paper not to adopt the trade and commercial language of "suppliers, consumption abroad, commercial presence" and so on. However, a more inclusive term is needed to acknowledge the diversity of actors who are delivering all levels of tertiary education, both domestically and internationally, and therefore the term providers is used. Yet it is also important to distinguish between the more traditional institutional providers and some of the alternative or new types of providers, many of whom are commercial for-profit in nature and purpose.

There is great confusion in the sector about the meaning and use of the three terms "transnational", "cross-border", and "borderless" education. All three have important distinguishing features. But, in the world of practice and policy, they are often used interchangeably and this causes some misunderstanding. In this paper, the newer term "cross-border education" will be used in order to emphasise the implications of crossing jurisdictional (regional, national, sub-regional) boundaries in terms of establishing/acknowledging legislation, policy and practice relating to quality assurance and accreditation of education programmes/institutions, and subsequently the recognition of qualifications.

Transnational education is a more established term and is used differently in various parts of the world. For instance, in Australia the term emerged as a way to differentiate between international students who were being recruited to Australian-based universities and those students who were being enrolled in Australian programmes offshore. In Europe, a subsidiary text to the Lisbon Recognition Convention has defined transnational education in terms of "the learner being located in a country different from the one where the awarding institution is based" (UNESCO/Council of Europe, 2001). This has been a helpful definition and is most useful when referring to the movement of programmes through franchise, twinning and distance education operations. A new question emerges with regard to cross-border education providers that are not "home-based" or part of a national education system and for the sake of a better term are "stateless". This raises the question of whether the learner is in fact located in a different country from the awarding institution.

The term "borderless education" first appeared in an Australian report by Cunningham et al. (2000) and was followed by a similar type of study in the United Kingdom. Basically, the term "borderless education" refers to the blurring of conceptual, disciplinary and geographic borders tradition-ally inherent in higher education (CVCP 2000). It is interesting to juxta-pose the concepts of borderless education and cross-border education. The former term acknowledges the disappearance of borders while the latter term actually emphasises the existence of borders. Both approaches reflect the reality of today. In this period of unprecedented growth in dis-tance and e-learning education, geographic borders seem to be of little consequence. Yet, on the other hand, we can detect a growing importance of borders when the focus turns to regulatory responsibility, especially related to quality assurance, funding and accreditation.

It is probably true (and even desirable) that cross-border will eventually be replaced by a term that will highlight the notion of national/interna-tional recognition rather than the nuance of national borders. However, this will take some time, as appropriate national, regional and interna-tional mechanisms need to be in place to ensure reliable, transparent and comparable recognition procedures. The discussion on the meaning of transnational, cross-border and borderless education is meant to illustrate how different countries/regions use the term, but also to signal that there are significant implications for how cross-border data is collected and how regulatory frameworks are created.

Examples of new developments in European cross-border education

In the past several years, European countries have been more active in cross-border education both in the recruitment of foreign students and also in offering programmes in other countries and establishing branch campuses. For instance, the Netherlands Business School (Universitiet Nijenrode) has recently opened a branch campus in Nigeria. Dubai has recently developed a "Knowledge Village" and to date the London School of Economics is one of the key providers of education along with India's Manipal Academy of Higher Education and the University of Wollongong from Australia. In Bahrain, a new Euro University is being planned in affiliation with the University of Hanover. The University of Westminster is the key foreign academic partner in the new private Kingdom University of Bahrain and plays a similar advisory/provision role with new institutions in Nigeria, Uzbekistan and Kazakhstan. Lastly, a good example of the complexity in partnerships is the franchise agree-ment where the distance MBA programme of Heriot-Watt University from the United Kingdom is being offered through the American University in Egypt. The United Kingdom is the most active cross-border provider in Europe with over 100,000 students enrolled in programmes offered overseas. These are but a few examples of hundreds of initiatives that involve European universities offering programmes in other countries.[65]

In terms of cross-border activities by private companies and other foreign providers offering programmes in Europe, it is interesting to note that US-based Laureate Education (formerly Sylvan Learning System) owns a part of or all of the Universidad Europea de Madrid in Spain, Les Roches and Glion Hotel School in Switzerland and the Ecole Supérieure du Commerce Extérieur de Paris in France. Apollo International and Webster University from the United States are offering courses in the Netherlands, and Raffles La Salle from Singapore has recently signed an agreement with Middlesex University to offer their bachelor's and master's programmes in fashion and design. Finally, Kaplan, another US company, has recently purchased the Dublin Business School. These examples illustrate the growing interest in private for-profit companies to establish a presence in Europe either by providing courses through satellite operations or by purchasing existing higher education institutions.

In short, there is ample evidence that in addition to the significant movement of academic programmes within Europe, there is growing interest by European higher education institutions to offer their programmes to other regions of the world. And finally foreign private companies see Europe as a lucrative education market and are expanding their presence in several European countries. These new developments have significant implications for quality assurance of academic programmes and the recognition of qualifications and will be discussed in the following sections.

Complexities and challenges of cross-border provision

There is a new level of complexity in recognising qualifications that are offered by non-domestic institutions/providers. The recognition of a qualification is usually based on a national system which registers/licences the education institution/provider and, secondly, requires a quality assurance assessment or accreditation for the programmes and/or for the institution/provider. In the past decade, many countries in Europe and elsewhere have established some type of governmental or non-governmental evaluation/accreditation system. This is a significant accomplishment. However, many of the new and existing systems are appropriately oriented to the recognition of qualifications offered by traditional domestic institutions. They are not equipped yet to register/license or assess the

---

68. All examples and statistics have been taken from the Reports and Breaking News Service of the Observatory for Borderless Education in the United Kingdom: http://www.obhe.ac.uk

quality of cross-border programmes and qualifications offered by foreign institutions and providers, some of whom are private for-profit companies. The development of this capacity is an important challenge and undertaking for the next decade. New mechanisms and frameworks at regional and international levels also need to be considered to complement and strengthen the capacity of national level governmental, non-governmental and professional bodies with this challenge.

Diversity of providers – traditional and alternative

Traditional higher education institutions are no longer the only deliverers of academic courses and programmes at home or across borders. International conglomerates, media and IT companies and new partnerships of private and public bodies are increasingly engaged in the provision of education both domestically and internationally. The term provider is used as a generic term to include all types of higher education institutions as well as companies and networks involved in cross-border education.

Chart One presents a proposed typology of cross-border providers. It is an attempt to conceptually map the diversity of actors and to separate the type of provider from the form of cross-border delivery. The key factors used to describe each category of provider and to distinguish one category from another are:

–   recognised by a bona fide national licensing/accrediting body;

–   part of a national "home" higher education system;

–   public, private or religious;

–   non-profit or for-profit.

The proposed typology is purposely rather generic and does not provide specific details on the characteristics of each category of provider. The typology is oriented to international academic provision but may have some relevance for domestic delivery as well. There seems to be a continual flow of announcements about new providers and new forms of partnerships between providers. It is an evolving field that needs to be monitored and this is why the typology is a work in progress.

Chart One: Typology of cross-border/international providers

Category	Status	Orientation	Notes
Recognised HEIs	Can be public, private or religious institutions. Usually part of home national education system and recognised by national bona fide licensing/accrediting body.	Can be non-profit or profit-oriented.	Known as traditional type of HEI focusing on teaching, research and service.
Non-recognised HEIs	Usually private and not formally part of national education system. Includes HEIs that provide a course of study but are not recognised by national bona fide licensing/accreditation body. If the non-recognised HEIs are of low quality they are often referred to as "rogue" providers.	Usually profit-oriented but can be non-profit as well.	"Diploma mills" sell degrees but do not provide programmes of study and are related to cross-border education but are not a true provider. "Rogue providers" are often accredited by agencies that are selling accreditations (accreditation mills) or by self-accrediting groups or companies.
Commercial company HEIs	Can be publicly traded company (see Global Education Index of OBHE) or privately owned. Includes: 1. companies that establish HEIs that may or may not be "recognised" by bona fide licensing/accrediting bodies; and 2. companies that focus more on the provision of services. Usually not part of "home" national education system.	Profit oriented.	Known as type of "alternative or new provider" Can include variety of companies (e.g. media, IT, publishing) who provide education programmes and support services. Can complement, co-operate, compete or co-exist with more traditional HEIs. Known as type of "alternative or new provider".
Corporate HEIs May be difficult to identify home country	Not part of home national education system. Usually part of major international corporation and outside national education system. Not usually recognised by national bona fide licensing/accreditation body.	Not relevant.	Often collaborate with traditional HEIs especially for degree awarding power.
Professional, governmental, and non-governmental organisations and networks	Can be individual or a combination of public/public or public/private or private/private organisations and HEIs. The organisations/networks may or may not be part of home national education system; and they may or may not be recognised by national bona fide licensing/accreditation body. However, some of the individual partners may be.	Usually profit-oriented in purpose.	Known as type of "alternative or new provider".
Virtual HEIs	Includes HEIs that are 100% virtual. May or may not be part of home national education system and may or may not be recognised by national bona fide licensing/ accreditation body.	Usually profit oriented if delivering cross-border.	Difficult for receiving national education system to monitor or regulate international virtual HEIs due to distance delivery methods.
Footnotes	*Home country means country of origin or sending/source country. Host country means receiving country.*		*Traditional HEIs are differentiated from the alternative and new types of companies/ providers that are being established.*

Source: Knight 2005.

One of the central issues in looking at the typology of providers is who recognises and gives the provider the power to award the qualifications in the "home or sending country" and/or in the "host or receiving country". However, as previously pointed out, some of the "alternative or new providers" are not part of or are not recognised by a "home" national education system. What does this mean, then, for the international recognition of their degrees or diplomas? Another challenge in developing a typology is that the terms "public", "private" and "religious" are interpreted and used in different ways among countries (and sometimes within countries as well). The emergence of new trade regulations applying to education services usually means that all commercial cross-border providers are considered to be private by host/receiving country regardless of their status at home. This adds yet another complicating dimension to the task.

Different modes of mobility - programme and provider

The different forms of programme and provider mobility introduce yet another level of complexity. To date, much of the discussion about programme and provider mobility has consciously or unconsciously linked the type of provider with a certain mode of delivery. This has been a contributing factor to the general state of confusion about recognising providers and programmes. Therefore, it is important to separate the type of provider from the mode of cross-border delivery. Secondly, it is helpful to distinguish between whether it is a course/programme being delivered in another country or whether the provider itself is moving as this has implications for quality assurance, accreditation and recognition of qualifications.

Programme mobility

Cross-border mobility of programmes can be described as:

> "the movement of individual education/training courses and programmes across national/regional borders through face to face, distance or a combination of these modes. Credits towards a qualification can be awarded by the sending foreign country provider or by an affiliated domestic partner or jointly."

Chart Two: Typology of cross-border programme mobility modes

Category	Description	Comments
Franchise	An arrangement whereby a provider in the source country A authorises a provider in another country B to deliver its course/programme/service in country B or other countries. The qualification is awarded by provider in country A.	Arrangements for teaching, management, assessment, profit-sharing, awarding of credit/qualification etc. are customised for each franchise arrangement.
Twinning	A situation whereby a provider in source country A collaborates with a provider located in country B to develop an artic-ulation system allowing students to take course credits in country B and/or source country A. Only one qualification is awarded by provider in source country A.	Arrangements for twinning programmes and awarding of degree usually comply with national regulations of the provider in the source country A.
Double/joint degree	An arrangement whereby providers in different countries collaborate to offer a programme for which a student receives a qualification from each provider or a joint award from the collaborating providers.	Arrangements for programme provision and criteria for awarding the qualifications are customised for each collaborative initiative in accordance with national regulations.
Articulation	Various types of articulation arrange-ments between providers in different countries permit students to gain credit for courses/programmes offered/ delivered by collaborating providers.	Allows students to gain credit for work done with a provider other than the provider awarding the qualification.
Validation	Validation arrangements between providers in different countries which allow provider B in receiving country to award the qualification of provider A in source country.	In some cases, the source country provider may not offer these courses or awards itself.
Virtual/distance	Arrangements where providers deliver courses/programme to students in differ-ent countries through distance and on line modes. May include some face-to-face support for students through domes-tic study or support centres.	

Source: Knight 2005.

A key factor in programme mobility is "who" awards the course credits or ultimate credential for the programme. As the movement of pro-grammes proliferates, there will undoubtedly be further changes to national, regional and even international regulatory frameworks. The question of "who grants the credits/awards" will be augmented by "who recognises the provider" and whether or not the programme has been "accredited or quality-assured" by a bona fide body. Of critical impor-tance is whether the qualification is recognised for employment or further study in the receiving country and in other countries as well. The per-ceived legitimacy, recognition and ultimate mobility of the qualification are fundamental issues yet to be resolved.

147

Given that several modes of programme mobility involve partnerships, there are questions about who owns the intellectual property rights to course curriculum and materials. What are the legal and moral roles and responsibilities of the participating partners in terms of academic, staffing, recruitment, evaluation, financial, and administrative matters? While the movement of programmes across borders has been taking place for many years, it is clear that the new types of providers, partnerships, awards and delivery modes are challenging national and international policies and regulatory frameworks and that there are more questions than answers at the present time.

Provider mobility

Cross-border mobility of provider can be described as "the physical or virtual movement of an education provider across a national/regional border to establish a presence to provide education/training programmes and/or services to students and other clients". The difference between programme and provider mobility is one of scope and volume in terms of programmes/services offered and the local presence (and investment) by the foreign provider. Credits and qualifications are awarded by the foreign provider (through foreign, local or self-accreditation methods) or by an affiliated domestic partner or jointly. Forms of cross-border provider mobility include branch campuses, mergers with or acquisitions of domestic providers, independent institutions, study and support centres plus other types of innovative affiliations. A distinguishing feature between programme and provider mobility is that with provider mobility the learner is not necessarily located in a different country from the awarding institution.

Chart Three: Typology of cross-border provider mobility modes

Category	Description	Examples
Branch campus	Provider in country A establishes a satellite campus in country B to deliver courses and programmes to students in country B (may also include country A students taking a semester/courses abroad). The qualification awarded is from provider in country A.	Netherlands Business School has a branch campus in Nigeria and the University of Indianapolis has a branch campus in Athens.
Independent institution	Foreign provider A (a traditional university, a commercial company or alliance/network) establishes in country B a stand-alone HEI to offer courses /programmes and awards.	The German University in Cairo.
Acquisition/merger	Foreign provider A purchases a part of or 100% of local HEI in country B.	Laureate (formerly Sylvan Learning Systems) has merged with and/or purchased local HEIs in Spain, France and Switzerland.
Study centre/ teaching site	Foreign provider A establishes study centres in country B to support students taking their courses/programmes. Study centres can be independent or in collaboration with local providers in country B.	Texas A&M has a "university centre" in Mexico City. Troy University (US) has an MBA teaching site in Bangkok.
Affiliation /networks (collaborative provision)	Different types of "public and private", "traditional and new" providers from various countries collaborate through innovative types of partnerships to establish networks/ institutions to deliver courses and programmes in local and foreign countries through distance or face-to-face modes.	Partnership between the Captor Group and Carnegie Mellon University to establish campus in India.
Virtual university	Provider that delivers credit courses and degree programmes to students in different countries through distance education modes and that generally does not have face-to-face support services for students.	International Virtual University, Hibernia College, Arab Open University.

Source: Knight 2005.

The increase in different types of cross-border providers includes non-traditional or alternative types of institutions/providers that are not part of any national education system and are in essence "stateless". Therefore, the advantage of knowing the status of the provider in their "home" country does not apply to these types of providers. As a result, they are "unknown" entities in terms of quality of the education course/programme and the acceptance/trustworthiness of their awards. One common response to "not being part of a national education system" is to obtain "accreditation status" from different types of accreditation bodies or agencies. This in turn leads to the question of whether the accreditation agency is bona fide and can be trusted.

Diversity of accreditors – recognised and rogue

The increased awareness of the need for quality assurance and/or accreditation has lead to several new developments in accreditation, some of which are helping the task of domestic and international recognition of qualifications, some of which are only serving to hinder and complicate matters.

First, it is important to acknowledge the efforts of many countries to establish criteria and procedures for quality assurance recognition systems and the approval of bona fide accreditors. At the same time, it is necessary to recognise the increase in self-appointed and rather self-serving accreditors, as well as accreditation mills that simply sell "bogus" accreditation labels.

The desire for accreditation status is leading to a commercialisation of quality assurance/accreditation as programmes and providers strive to gain as many "accreditation" stars as possible in order to increase competitiveness and perceived international legitimacy. The challenge is how to distinguish between bona fide and rogue accreditors, especially when neither the cross-border provider nor the accreditor are nationally based or recognised as part of a national higher education system.

A second aspect of the race for accreditation is the growth in the international dimension, or perhaps more aptly put, the international market for accreditation. First, it is important to acknowledge the upside of the internationalisation of accreditation. New initiatives for mutual recognition of accreditation processes among countries, especially in the regulated professionals, have been a positive development. Countries lacking fully developed quality assurance systems have also benefited from the assistance of foreign bona fide accreditors. However, there are also instances when commercial and competitiveness motives have fuelled the desire for more accreditation stars, resulting in inappropriate and non-reliable quality assurance processes. While this can apply to both cross-border and domestic provision, it is particularly worrisome for cross-border provision as attention to national policy objectives and cultural orientation is often neglected. In both cases, there is no clear understanding if the accreditor is bona fide and if the qualifications will be able to be acceptable for academic or professional purposes.

New types of collaborative arrangements

The diversity of new types of providers has lead to more innovative and complex collaborative arrangements for the delivery of education programmes and degrees. The combination of partners (local/foreign, traditional and new providers, recognised/not-recognised, private/public, non-profit/for-profit) results in major difficulties in determining whose study programme is being offered, who is responsible for delivery, who is ultimately granting the qualification and most importantly, who has licensed and quality-assured the programme/provider.

These are some of the realities of cross-border movement of programmes and providers that have significant implications for the qualify assurance of programmes and providers and consequently for the ultimate recognition of qualification for academic and professional purposes.

Issues and implications

The typologies of cross-border providers and the different means and arrangements for providing education across national/regional boundaries illustrate the diversity of actors, types of provision, delivery methods and of course rationales, driving the whole enterprise of cross-border education. This section focuses primarily on the issues that relate to recognition of providers, programmes and credits/qualifications at national, regional and international levels.

At the current time, there are five macro-issues that are receiving the most attention and which have different dimensions and consequences for the various types of providers. These issues are interrelated and all are influenced by regulations of the sending and the receiving country. The first issue is the licensing or registering of institutions/providers who are delivering across borders courses/programmes and hence qualifications. Are they recognised and part of the home national system and also recognised/licensed in the receiving country? The second issue focuses on the quality of the courses/programmes being offered and the quality of the academic experience of the student. The third issue follows on the same theme and focuses on the role of accreditation and the more recent trends of internationalisation and commercialisation of accreditation for worldwide status and profile, rather than for standards. The fourth issue addresses the recognition of the actual award or qualification being offered for purposes of employment and further study. This point relates directly to the importance of student/employer and public being aware of the quality and validity of the programmes and awards provided. The fifth issue focuses on the challenge and need for a review of the policy and regulatory environments in which programme and provider mobility is operating.

Registration and licensing of foreign providers

A fundamental question is whether the institutions, companies and networks that are delivering award-based programmes are registered, licensed or recognised by the receiving country. The answer to this question varies.

151

There are many countries that do not have the regulatory systems in place to register out-of-country providers. Several reasons account for this, including lack of capacity or political will. If providers are not registered or recognised it is difficult to monitor their performance. It is usual practice, that if an institution/provider is not registered as part of a national system, then regulatory frameworks for quality assurance or accreditation do not apply. This is the situation in many countries in the world and hence foreign providers (bona fide and rogue) do not have to comply with national regulations of the receiving countries.

The questions and factors at play in the registration or licensing of foreign providers are many. For instance, are the criteria or conditions applicable to those providers who are part of and recognised by a national education system in their home country different from those for providers who are not? Does it make a difference if the provider is for-profit or non-profit, private or public, an institution or a company? What conditions apply if in fact the provider is a company that has no home-based presence and only establishes institutions in foreign countries? How does one monitor partnerships between local domestic institutions/companies and foreign ones? Is it even possible to register a completely virtual provider? Clearly, there are challenges and difficulties involved in trying to establish appropriate and effective national or regional regulatory systems for registration of non-domestic providers.

Often there are bilateral cultural/academic agreements in place to facilitate and monitor the foreign presence of education providers. However, the fact that education services are now part of bilateral and multilateral trade agreements introduces new regulations and challenges. The existence of trade agreements that aim to liberalise and promote trade in education services is a relatively recent factor to be considered. Trade agreements can help to provide new opportunities, but also present new dilemmas. A key question facing national governments, as well as international organisations, is to what extent will the introduction of new national regulations to license or recognise out-of-country providers be interpreted as barriers for trade and therefore need to be modified to comply with trade policies.

All and all, the issue of regulating and licensing providers that deliver education across borders needs further attention. Consideration of what national, regional and international policies and frameworks are necessary and feasible in light of new trade regulations merits study by the education sector. This is becoming a complex and more urgent issue to address.

Assessing and ensuring quality assurance

If we thought the questions related to registration and licensing were complex, matters become even more complicated when one looks at accreditation and quality assurance of programmes and providers moving across national/regional jurisdictional borders. The terms "accreditation" and "quality assurance" have different meaning and significance depending on the country, actor or stakeholder using them. For the purposes of this discussion, quality recognition and assurance is used in a general sense and includes quality audit, evaluation, accreditation and other review processes and elements.

Firstly, it must be noted that increased importance has certainly been given to quality assurance at the institutional level and at the national level in the past decade. Quality assurance mechanisms and national organisations have been developed in over sixty countries in the last decade. New regional quality networks have also been established. The primary task of these groups has been to assess and assure the quality of domestic higher education provision of public and private higher education institutions. However, the increase in cross-border education by institutions and commercial companies has introduced a new challenge to the field of quality assurance. Historically, national quality assurance agencies have generally not focused their efforts on assessing the quality of imported and exported programmes, with some notable exceptions. Hong Kong, Malaysia, South Africa and Israel, as receivers of cross-border providers and programmes, have developed regulatory systems to register and monitor the quality of foreign provision. The United Kingdom and Australia are examples of sending countries that have introduced quality assurance for exported cross-border provision by their recognised HEIs. The question now facing the sector is how to deal with the increase in cross-border education by public/private institutions, and in particular by the new private commercial companies and providers who are not part of or recognised by nationally-based quality assurance schemes. Is it feasible and desirable that the new and alternative types of internationally oriented higher education providers become quality-assured or accredited by the existing national/regional bodies that evaluate the more traditional types of public and private universities? Or will alternative type of evaluation and accreditation procedures be developed to respond to their particular characteristics, rationales and issues?

It is probable that sectors in addition to education will be interested in developing international quality standards and procedures for education. ISO standards, or other industry-based mechanisms such as the Baldridge Awards, are examples of quality systems that might be applied or modelled

153

for cross-border education. The education sector has mixed views on the appropriateness of quality standards being established for education by those outside the sector; some see merit to this idea and others see problems. At the same time, there are divergent opinions on the desirability and value of any international standards or criteria for quality assurance as this might jeopardise the sovereignty of national level systems or contribute to standardisation, not necessarily quality standards. This issue is complex and there are many different actors and stakeholders involved. However, given the realities of today's growth in the number and types of cross-border education providers there is a sense of urgency to the question of how to ensure the quality of imported and exported education providers and programmes.

Accreditation – commercialisation and internationalisation?

Market forces are making the profile and reputation of an institution/provider and their courses more and more important. Major investments are being made in marketing and branding campaigns in order to get name recognition and to increase enrolments. The possession of some type of accreditation is part of the campaign and assures prospective students that the programmes/awards are of high standing. This is introducing an internationalisation and even commercialisation dimension to accreditation practices. However, it is very important not to confuse commercial bona fide accreditation agencies with "accreditation mills".

It is interesting to note the increase in the number of bona fide national and international accreditation agencies which are now working in over 50 countries. For instance, the US national and regional accrediting bodies are providing/selling their services in over 65 countries. The same trend is discernible for accreditation bodies of the professions, such as ABET (Engineering) from the US and EQUIS (Business) from Europe.

At the same time, there are networks of institutions and new organisations that are self-appointed and engage in accreditation of their members. These are positive developments when seen through the lens of trying to improve the quality of the academic offer. However, there is some concern that they are not totally objective in their assessments and may be more interested in contributing to the race for more and more accreditation "stars" than to improving quality. Another related development that is more worrisome is the growth in accreditation mills. These organisations are not recognised or legitimate bodies and they more or less "sell" accreditation status without any independent assessment. They are similar to degree mills that sell certificates and degrees with little or no coursework. Different education stakeholders, especially the students, employers and the public need to be aware of these accreditation (and degree) mills, which are often no more than a web address and are therefore outside the jurisdiction of national regulatory systems.

Recognition of qualifications

The need to have mechanisms that recognise academic and professional qualifications gained through domestic or international delivery of education is another important consequence of increased cross-border activity. The key questions are who awards the qualification (especially in collaborative provision arrangements and for private company providers), is the provider recognised, if so by what kind of accrediting/licensing body, and in what country is that body located? Given the importance of both student mobility and professional labour mobility, within and between countries, the mechanisms for qualification recognition have to be national, regional and or international in nature and application.

UNESCO has long acknowledged the requirement of an international system to facilitate and ensure recognition of academic and professional qualifications. Regional UNESCO conventions on the recognition of qualifications were established more than twenty-five years ago and have been ratified by over 100 member states in Africa, Asia and the Pacific, the Arab states, Europe and Latin America. They are unique legally binding instruments dealing with cross-border mutual recognition of qualifications. There is limited awareness of these instruments except for the European regional convention, which in 1997 was updated jointly by the Council of Europe and UNESCO in the form of the Lisbon Recognition Convention. However, the Convention will only be most effective if there are national level regulations and capacity to implement and monitor it. There is significant room for improvement in the implementation of the Lisbon Recognition Convention in many European countries and the other regional conventions need to be updated in light of the changes and growth in cross-border education.

The credibility of higher education programmes and qualifications is extremely important for students, employers, the public at large and of course for the academic community itself. Additional efforts are needed at institutional, national and international levels to keep the different stakeholders cognisant of new opportunities for education and professional mobility but at the same time aware of the new risks such as rogue providers, and diploma and accreditation mills and the more subtle issues related to alternative and new providers and new qualifications. The most critical issue is assurance that the qualification awarded is legitimate and

155

will be recognised for employment purposes or for further studies either at home or abroad. This is a major challenge facing the national and international higher education sector at the present time.

National, regional and international frameworks

Of current interest and debate is whether national-level accreditation and quality assurance systems (where they exist) are able to attend to the complicating factors of education mobility across countries, cultures and jurisdictional systems. A fundamental question is whether countries have the capacity and political will to establish and monitor quality systems for both incoming and outgoing education programmes given the diversity of providers and delivery methods. Should national quality/accreditation systems be complemented and augmented by regional or international frameworks? Is it advisable and feasible to develop mutual recognition systems between and among countries? Would an international code of good practice for cross-border provision be appropriate or strong enough to monitor quality? These are key questions for the education sector to address. As the discussion moves forward it will be of strategic and substantive importance to recognise the roles and responsibilities of all the players involved in quality assurance including individual institutions/providers, national quality assurance systems, non-government and independent accreditation bodies, and regional/international organisations. It will be important to work in a collaborative and complementary fashion to build a system that ensures the quality and integrity of cross-border education and maintains the confidence of society in higher education.

International developments related to recognition of qualifications and cross-border education

UNESCO/OECD joint initiatives

Both UNESCO and the OECD have identified the accelerated growth and increasing importance of cross-border education as a priority area for the higher education sector. The changes in the landscape of cross-border education present important new opportunities and potential risks. Individually the organisations are undertaking initiatives in the form of Global Forum meetings, expert working groups and new publications. Important outcomes of these activities are two new joint projects. They are:

- the UNESCO/OECD Guidelines for Quality Provision in Cross-border Higher Education; and

- the UNESCO/OECD Information Tool on Recognised Higher Education Institutions.

The purpose of the Joint Guidelines is to "ensure that the quality of cross-border provision of higher education is managed appropriately to limit low quality provision and rogue providers and to encourage these forms of cross-border delivery of higher education that provides new opportunities, wide access and increases the possibilities of improving the skills of individual students". A key assumption and intention of the guidelines is that quality provision is a fundamental way to protect students who are seeking and participating in cross-border education.

The Joint Guidelines are based on the principle of mutual trust and respect among countries and recognise the importance of national authority and activity in education policy making. The guidelines make recommendations for six key stakeholder groups: national governments, higher education institutions/providers, student groups, quality assurance and accreditation agencies, credential and qualification evaluation groups and professional bodies.

The guidelines are an important step towards increasing the awareness of key education actors and beneficiaries of the new opportunities, risks, and challenges of cross-border education. As guidelines, they are without any regulatory power, but they are critical to ensuring that cross-border education provision is a priority issue and receives attention and action by key stakeholders.

A second joint activity is the development of an "Information Tool on Recognised Higher Education Institutions". This is an important adjunct to the guidelines and will provide concrete information about higher education institutions that are recognised by a competent body in participating countries. Each country voluntarily supplies and is responsible for the reliability and currency of the information. Clearly there are many challenges involved in designing, implementing and updating such a tool in a field that is growing and changing at such fast pace. For instance, how does one define a higher/tertiary education institution? It is obvious that many providers of higher education are not traditional higher education institutions; will they be included? Secondly, the terms "recognised" and "competent body" often mean very different things in different countries, and therefore common reference points will need to found among the diverse interpretations. What kind of quality assurance or accreditation mechanisms are necessary to be acknowledged by a country as a "recognised institution" and therefore to be included in the "international information tool"? The ability of many countries to produce and update this kind of list on national institutions, let alone cross-border providers, is still lacking and will necessitate national capacity-building strategies. It is clear that a simple list of "recognised institutions" is not enough. A consensus is needed on what supplementary information is desirable and feasible. The benefits of such a tool are many, and so are the challenges in developing and updating it; however, it is an important and welcome step and contribution to the field. The critical questions about the quality and recognition of those education providers that are outside a national education system still remain and hopefully will be addressed by these working groups.

Concluding remarks

Europe has put in place important mechanisms to ensure fair and transparent recognition of qualifications so that credentials earned in one European country are recognised and valid for further studies and employment in other countries within Europe. These tools include the Lisbon Recognition Convention, the Code of Good Practice in the Provision of Transnational Education, the ENIC and NARIC Networks and centres and the Diploma Supplement, all of which can contribute to the regulation and adoption of good practice for recognising qualifications. New initiatives such as national qualifications frameworks and the proposed pan-European Qualifications Framework are also central to an improved process for the recognition of qualifications. These efforts are to be applauded. However, the widespread implementation of recognition policies at institutional, national and regional levels remains a challenge. It is even more of a challenge when one considers the complexities attached to the recognition of awards for programmes being delivered out of Europe and for programmes that are being imported into Europe, especially by new and alternative types of providers.

The growth in the volume, scope and dimensions of cross-border education has the potential to provide increased access, and to promote innovation and responsiveness of higher education, but it also brings new challenges and unexpected consequences. There are the realities that unrecognised and rogue cross-border providers are active; that much of the latest cross-border education provision is being driven by commercial interests and gain; that mechanisms to recognise qualifications and ensure quality of the academic course/programme are still not established in many countries and that new alternative providers do not have access to them in those countries where they are in place. These present major challenges to the education sector. It is important to acknowledge the huge potential of cross-border education but not at the expense of academic quality or the recognition of qualifications for both academic and professional work at home and abroad.

References

Adam, S. (2001). "Transnational Education". A study prepared for the Confederation of European Union Rectors' Conferences. Geneva, Switzerland.

Coleman, D. (2003). "Quality Assurance in Transnational Education", in *Journal of Studies in International Education*, vol. 7, no. 4, pp. 354-78.

Garrett, R. and L. Verbik (2004). "Transnational delivery by UK Higher Education. Part 1: data and missing data". Observatory on Borderless Higher Education. London, UK.

Garrett, R. (2003). "Mapping the Education Industry. Part Two: Public Companies – relationships with higher education." Observatory on Borderless Higher Education. London, UK.

IDP (2002). *The Global Student Mobility 2025 Report.* IDP Australia, Canberra, Australia.

Kaufmann, Chantal (2001). "The recognition of transnational education qualifications". Paper prepared for Seminar on Transnational Education, Malmö, Sweden.

Knight, J. (2005). *Crossborder Education: Programs and Providers on the Move. Research Monograph.* Canadian Bureau for International Education. Ottawa, Canada.

Knight, J. (2004). "Internationalization Remodeled: Rationales, Strategies and Approaches", in *Journal for Studies in International Education.* Vol. 8 no. 1.

Knight, J. (2004). "Crossborder Education: The Complexities of Globalization, Internationalization and Trade", Chapter 5 in Internationalisation and Quality Assurance. SAUVCA, Pretoria, South Africa.

Knight, J. (2003). *GATS, Trade and Higher Education. Perspectives 2003 – Where are we?* Observatory on Borderless Higher Education. London, UK.

Machados dos Santos, S. (2000). "Introduction to the theme of Transnational Educational Services". Presented at the Conference of Directors General for Higher Education and Heads of the Rectors' Conferences of the European Union. Aveiro, Portugal.

Middlehurst, R. and S. Woodfield (2003). "The Role of Transnational, Private and For-Profit Provision in Meeting Global Demand for Tertiary Education: Mapping, Regulation and Impact". Report for the Commonwealth of Learning and UNESCO.

Middlehurst, R. (2002). "The developing world of borderless higher education: markets, providers, quality assurance and qualification". Working Paper for UNESCO First Global Forum on International Quality Assurance, Accreditation and the Recognition of Qualifications in Higher Education. UNESCO. Paris, France.

OECD (2004a). *Internationalisation and trade in higher education – challenges and opportunities*. Organisation for Economic Co-operation and Development. Paris, France.

OECD (2004b). *Quality and recognition in higher education: the cross-border challenge*. Organisation for Economic Co-operation and Development. Paris, France.

UNESCO (2002). *Globalization and the market in higher education: quality, accreditation and qualifications*. UNESCO/Economica. Paris, France.

UNESCO/OECD (2004a). Annex on "Guidelines for Quality Provision in Cross-border Higher Education". UNESCO and OECD. Paris, France.

UNESCO/OECD (2004b). Draft Proposal on "Proposed next steps for an international information tool on recognised higher education institutions". Paris, France.

The United States
as a stakeholder in the Bologna Process

Timothy S. Thompson

> *As Stanford University economist Paul Romer has long argued, great advances have always come from ideas. Ideas do not fall from the sky; they come from people. People write software. People design products. People start the new businesses. Every new thing that gives us pleasure or productivity or convenience ... is the result of human ingenuity.*

> R. Florida

Whether as immigrants or temporarily as students, scholars or researchers, the United States has long received many benefits from people from other countries coming to the US. Indeed, the US owes its development as a nation to people from other countries and since the mid-nineteenth century, the US has been dependent on immigrant labour for much of its economic success. Some argue that the ability of the United States to be a centre of ingenuity and invention has been its open-ness to new ideas, especially in scientific fields, the arts, and entertain-ment. That openness in turn has fostered the research and development that has been a major economic engine and made the US a magnet for the world's best and brightest. But today there are clear indicators that the best and the brightest are looking at other parts of the globe as the incu-bators of new ideas. At the end of the day, the higher education commu-nity in the US will view itself as a stakeholder in the Bologna Process to the degree to which the United States is able to keep its doors open to stu-dents from other countries. There are challenges to keeping the doors open. This chapter takes a look at those challenges.

Post-secondary education in the United States

Post-secondary academic and professional education in the United States is primarily offered in two types of institutions, colleges and universities. At the undergraduate level (the level leading to a bachelor's degree) and in terms of programme of study, there is no distinction between a college and a university. Both offer programmes of study leading to the bachelor's degree. Distinctions between a college and a university are generally a matter of the size of the institution (number of students and faculty) and

161

that universities also offer graduate degrees, the master's degree and the doctoral degree, although not all universities offer programmes of study leading to the PhD. However, the distinctions in name can be confusing. For example Denison University in Ohio offers no graduate degrees and carries the name university as an historical appellation, not as an indicator that Denison University offers both undergraduate and graduate degrees.

To add to the complexity just a little, a community college differs from a college in that the community college offers among a variety of programmes of study, an academic programme of study leading to an associate degree. In many cases, the associate degree programme of study at a community college will have an articulation agreement with a college or university in the region where the community college is located that enables a student to transfer credit from the associate degree programme to a programme of study leading to a bachelor's degree.

Recognition of academic qualifications

The organisational features of academic post-secondary education in the US point to another feature of post-secondary or higher education in the United States. Whether public or private, there is no centralised national government entity with authority for education in the United States. The US Department of Education is not our ministry of education. The absence of a federal educational authority is due in large part to the absence of education being mentioned in the US Constitution. With no federal education authority or ministry of education in the United States, institutions of higher education are autonomous. The control and authority rests with the institutions themselves or in some cases with individual states, as is generally the case of public state institutions, although public state institutions are still autonomous. This feature of higher education in the United States is reflected in Article II of the Lisbon Convention, where the competent authority in matters pertaining to the recognition of academic qualifications lies with the institution and not national or regional government authorities.

With no national authority in education, a critical component of post-secondary education in the US that establishes the framework for standard setting and a high degree uniformity in the organisation and recognition of degrees offered at institutions is the system of institutional and programme accreditation. The general public tends to be captivated by the highly subjective and "public relations/marketing" orientation of the ranking of institutions in the US. However, the objective core of an institution's standards, quality control, and assessment of an institution's ability to deliver the education reflected in its mission statement is its institutional accreditation by one of the regional accrediting bodies and the programme accreditation by one of the professional accrediting bodies such as the Accreditation Board for Engineering and Technology (ABET).

Although there is no central federal authority and therefore no government authority in matters of recognition of academic qualifications, until December 1968 the US Office of Education (predecessor of the US Department of Education) did provide guidance in the evaluation of foreign educational credentials to assist institutions in the process of admitting students from other countries to institutions in the US. However, the opinions expressed were offered as advice, not as governmental decisions or policies.

The National Council on the Evaluation of Foreign Educational Credentials

In the mid-1950s, a committee was formed with representation from the American Association of Collegiate Registrars and Admissions Officers, the Association of American Colleges, the Association of Graduate Schools, the Institute of International Education, and the National Association of Foreign Student Advisors, and with observers from the following: the American Council on Education, Commission on Education and International Affairs, the College Entrance Examination Board, the US Department of State, and the US Office of Education. That committee became the National Council on the Evaluation of Foreign Educational Credentials. Since its founding in the 1950s, the role of the Council has been to provide guidelines through providing Council recommendations for the interpretation of foreign academic credentials for the purpose of placement in educational and other institutions in the United States. The following, taken from a 1958 report on education in Korea, reveals the mission and purpose of the Council:

> "The Committee felt a need for co-ordinating the opinion of all groups interested in the placement of foreign students, so its first act was to arrange meetings which resulted in the organization of a Council on the Evaluation of Foreign Student Credentials…[the] Committee invited individuals on United States campuses to prepare factual reports on educational developments in various countries ….These reports, while in manuscript, are reviewed by the Council on Evaluation and the Council incorporates into each report recommendations regarding academic placement of foreign students coming into United States educational institutions. The following report on the Republic of Korea is intended to help admissions officers to arrive at their own decisions on proper and equitable placement of individual students. Admissions officers should, of course, give due consideration to the purposes, organization, and requirements of their own institutions, and to the academic and personal needs of each student concerned." (Koenig, 1958)

Although there have been many changes since its creation in 1955, the Council maintains its unique role as the only interassociational body in the United States offering standards for interpreting foreign educational credentials and for the purpose of assisting educational institutions in admitting and placing students primarily in academic programmes of study. However, it is important to underscore that the recommendations of the Council are provided as advisory opinions, the Council's recommendations are not statements of national policy and some of the recommendations of the Council have not been without controversy.

Multiple opinions

Another dimension of the evaluation of foreign academic credentials in the United States is the role played by private credential evaluation services. Many institutions, employers, professional bodies, as well as government agencies rely on the resources, analysis and opinions offered by the private credential evaluation services. And recently, a national education association, the American Association of Collegiate Registrars and Admission Officers (AACRAO), has started its own credential evaluation service. While many of these credential evaluation services offer opinions that are frequently backed by comprehensive and focused research, like the recommendations of the Council, the opinions and evaluations offered are advisory and are not statements of national policy. The array of opinions and practices in the United States, the absence of a federal authority, policy, or voice in matters concerning the evaluation and recognition of academic qualifications from other countries can be very confusing when viewed from outside the United States. In addition, the autonomy of institutions in making decisions (or adopting the opinions of other entities, be they the recommendations of the Council or the opinion of a private credential evaluation service) does lead to widely varying practices and positions when it comes to the issue of evaluating education from other countries. This is a challenge that will influence the assessment of the new degrees in Europe by institutions in the US. Indeed, the diversity in the evaluation of foreign educational credential has always been a challenge in the United States and the main motivation for the creation the National Council on the Evaluation of Foreign Educational Credential in 1955.

Assessment of the new degrees in Europe

As noted, there are multiple voices and perspectives in matters of recognition and the evaluation of academic credentials in the United States. There is no national authority that sets policy. Institutions are completely autonomous in making assessments about credentials from other countries. It is fully anticipated that there will be multiple opinions and decisions about the new degrees initiated under the Bologna Process. Some institutions may adopt the position that the new bachelor's degree representing three years of study cannot be viewed as equivalent to a four-year bachelor's degree. Other institutions may adopt the view that the new bachelor's degree can be viewed as appropriate preparation for admission to graduate-level studies at their institution. Other institutions may adopt entirely different views.

One thing is certain: that there will be multiple opinions and perspectives in the United States regarding the new degrees. This multiplicity of opinions and perspectives will be a challenge as we attempt to maintain the flow of ideas through the mobility of students, scholars, researchers, and faculty.

It is anticipated that the National Council on the Evaluation of Foreign Educational Credentials will review manuscripts detailing the new degrees initiated under the Bologna Process. How the Council will view the new degrees cannot be anticipated. Regardless, the Council's recommendation will not be a mandate for institutions. Some institutions will reflect on the Council's recommendations and take them into consideration when making assessments. Other institutions will go in other directions. The multiplicity of opinions and actions based on those opinions has always been a challenge and will continue to be a challenge.

The repercussions of terrorism

People around the world applaud America's efforts to improve its own security. But what the world does not like is the arbitrary and sometimes brash methods the country has adopted in its own defence.

R. Florida

The United States likes to think of itself as a "melting pot" of ethnicities and cultures. However, we are reluctant to admit the xenophobia that has laced our history as a country. To cite just two examples, the anti-German sentiment in the United States during the First World War manifested itself in ways ranging from a general dislike of anything or anyone of German heritage to the policy issued by President Wilson in 1917 that required all German males fourteen and older not naturalised to register as alien enemies by 4 February 1918. The internment of Japanese-American citizens during the Second World War is another example. There are many more examples throughout the history of the United States that reveal this disturbing aspect of the American character.

To the credit of the current administration, the public was asked not to turn the acts of terrorism of 11 September 2001 into a religious war on Islam in the United States. Nevertheless, in the wake of the attacks on the US, individuals in the US of Middle Eastern ancestry have felt an extreme tension, if not harassment. The changes in policy ranging from the implementation of the Student and Exchange Visitor Information System (SEVIS) and visa application fees to the interview process and fingerprinting of those who enter the US are presenting the US as unwelcoming, if not hostile.

What many view as the restrictive policies put in place nominally in the interest of national security combined with the latent and overt xenophobia in the United States present a challenge to attracting people from other countries. The concern expressed by some is that the United States will not be able to recover its position of pre-eminence in education and research once the "war on terrorism" is over. Putting out the welcome mat once again will not signal the return of the flow of students, scholars, and talent to the United States. Some have predicted that a seriously diminished flow of students, scholars, and talent to the United States will have far-reaching and long-lasting negative consequences for the United States.

Opportunities and challenges

The climate that emerged in the United States in the aftermath of 11 September 2001 is only one factor that will influence the decision of individuals to look elsewhere in the world for opportunities. Today, there are opportunities in many other countries. The Internet and the globalisation of information and higher education are enabling individuals and institutions to have access to information and resources only dreamed of a few years ago. The sharing of ideas is no longer limited to place. Educational and research opportunities that were viewed as mainly available only in the United States are now available in other countries.

Institutions in the US see themselves as competing with each other for the best and the brightest. In addition, with no federal authority for education, there has been no collective national agenda or co-ordinated effort in matters relating to the process of attracting students from other countries. By contrast, institutions in other countries are relying on "umbrella organisations" to promote all of the institutions in their country through various means, making it easier for students to apply to institutions in their countries.

In the absence of a clear and strong national voice or infrastructure, there is no mechanism in place for the US higher education community to speak with a collective voice and to influence the decisions of the government that impact on the flow of international students and scholars to the United States. Organisations such as NAFSA: Association of International Educators have been successful at times in influencing policies and procedures, but overall there is no strong collective voice raising concerns on behalf of the higher education community. The lack of a clear voice will be another challenge to be faced.

Looking to the future

These observations on the present state of international educational exchange in the United States paint a bleak picture for the future. In light of the challenges facing the United States, it is hard to be optimistic. However, if the decisions regarding the assessment of the new degrees in Europe are carefully and deliberately made in the context of keeping the doors open, how the new degrees are viewed may be an important first step. Continued dialogue and sharing of information will also contribute to keeping the doors open. And finally, the United States needs to be reminded that it is people who have been the source of new ideas and new ideas are the hope of the future.

References

Bollag, B. 2004. "Wanted: Foreign students." *Chronicle of Higher Education*, Vol. 51/7, p. A37

Field, K. 2004. "Fixing the visa quagmire." *Chronicle of Higher Education*, Vol. 51/7, p. A40.

Fletcher, A. and W. Smart. 1992. *Guide to Placement Recommendations: The National Council on the Evaluation of Foreign Educational Credentials*. Washington, D.C.: NAFSA.

Florida, R. 2004. "America's looming creativity crisis." *Harvard Business Review*, October, pp. 122-136.

Harty, L. 2004. "State Dept.: We don't want to lose even one student." *Chronicle of Higher Education*, Vol. 51/7, p. B 10.

Kless, S. 2004. "We threaten national security by discouraging the best and brightest students from abroad." *Chronicle of Higher Education*, Vol. 51/7, p. B9.

Koenig, C. 1958. *The Republic of Korea: A Guide to the Academic Placement of Students from the Republic of Korea in United States Education Institutions*. Washington, D.C.: AACRAO.

McCarthy, J. 2004. "Tapping the global student market." *IIE Networker*, Fall, 20-22.

Mooney, P., and S. Neelakantan. "No longer dreaming of America." *Chronicle of Higher Education*, Vol. 51/7, p. A41.

Wilson, R. 2004. "Settling for less." *Chronicle of Higher Education*, Vol. 51/7, p. A39.

Recognition 2010:
opportunities from which we cannot run away

Sjur Bergan

Predictions and years

Being asked to look at "Recognition 2010" is a challenge, to say the least. One is tempted to recall the words of the Danish humorist Piet Hein, who quipped that prediction is difficult, in particular about the future.[69] If the title of this chapter indicates a certain ambiguity, this is because I sense that many of our colleagues in the recognition field see opportunities ahead, but they are not entirely comfortable with all they see. Even in a brief chapter like this, I hope to explore some of the opportunities and, hopefully, lay some of the apprehensions to rest. My own apprehensions have as much to do with our attitudes to change as with the change itself.

It may also be worth reminding ourselves that it is sometimes difficult to distinguish predictions – indications of what is likely to happen – from our own desires for the future – what we would like to see happen. This is not to say, however, that we should throw our hands in the air and let things happen. Predictions are useful not least because they may help us identify likely developments as well as what action we might take to help those developments go in the direction we would like. We cannot always succeed, but we can always try. The chances of success, however, are greater if we adapt them to the prevailing environment than if we only base them on wishful thinking.

In thinking about 2010, it may also be useful to remember that some years have come to symbolise predictions in a particular way. The two in most recent memory are 1984 and 2000. The first gave us the adjective Orwellian, describing the kind of society that few of us would like to live in but that some less than tender souls may well long to rule over, while the second was connected with doom and gloom. Millenarian sects believed the world would come to an end and may well have been disappointed when it did not. Computer specialists were worried about another kind of apocalypse, but they were mostly relieved when the famous "2000 bug" did not materialise after all. 2010, then, is less dramatic and

---

69. Piet Hein's quips and aphorisms were published over a number of years as *Gruk*.

much more positive, for it has come to signify the establishment of the European Higher Education Area and, hence, the end of the Bologna Process.

By now, 1984 is history, 2000 is the still recent past and 2010 has moved from the realm of futurology to something that is much more comfortable to policy makers and bureaucrats: medium-term planning.

Considering recognition in 2010 from a European point of view is, then, considering what, in the medium term, the recognition community may do to help make the European Higher Education Area a reality only four years from now. This chapter will make no attempt at giving a complete overview of challenges, but it will seek to address six factors that I believe will be particularly important.

The legal framework

In a way, this is not a challenge. At European level, the legal framework is largely in place, through the Council of Europe/UNESCO Recognition Convention,[70] through subsidiary texts to this Convention and through the EU Directives on professional recognition. At least for most purposes of recognition, I believe we by and large have the legal instruments we need.

The main challenge will therefore lie in the implementation of the existing legal framework rather than in developing a new one, and this implementation will be the main focus of this chapter. As concerns further development of the legal framework, there are three areas where this may be required.

Firstly, while increasing the number of subsidiary texts to the Council of Europe/UNESCO Recognition Convention is no end in itself, there may still be issues that will require further texts of this kind. These issues will most likely have to do with recognition issues that were not fully covered by the Convention itself, in particular issues relating to qualifications that are not entirely a part of a national system. The Recommendation on the Recognition of Joint Degrees (adopted in 2004) and the Code of Good Practice in the Provision of Transnational Education (2001) are good examples of such texts, and further texts may be needed. The relationship between recognition and quality assurance is another area in which there have been important developments since the Convention was adopted, and where further standard setting texts may be required.

---

70. The full text of the Convention and its Explanatory Report, as well as a constantly updated list of signatures and ratifications, will be found at http://conventions.coe.int search for ETS No. 165.

Secondly, while the legal framework is largely in place at European level, this is not necessarily true at national level. Many countries have updated laws and regulations on recognition, and in some countries, any international treaty ratified by that country becomes part of national law. However, some countries have ratified the Convention without amending their national laws. All countries party to the Bologna Process should therefore review their own legislation to ensure that it is compatible with their obligations under the Convention.

Thirdly, the Council of Europe/UNESCO Recognition Convention is the first of what is often called the "new generation" of recognition conventions, and as such, it may serve as a model for other UNESCO regions of the world. While they would not copy the Convention, they may find the provisions of and experience with the Convention useful in updating their own legal framework. To my knowledge, the Arab Region has already come far in this respect, and work is also underway in the African Region. As we shall discuss later in the chapter, this is important to European countries because a common approach to recognition principles and methodology will facilitate the mutual recognition of qualifications.

Effects of laws in an internationalised environment

Laws are only effective if they are implemented and enforced. One could even question whether legal texts that are not enforced should be called laws, or whether they are rather guidelines for good practice – voluntary instruments that are certainly beneficial, but which are put into practice to the extent that people and institutions actually want to do so.

The point in our context is that, for the most part, law enforcement is linked to national authorities, national territories and national systems. There are exceptions to this, such as the legislation of the European Union and its European Court of Justice, the Council of Europe's European Convention and Court of Human Rights, the UN International Court of Justice and the now defunct Central American Court of Justice (1907-18), which is the earliest example of an international court of which this author is aware.[71] Nevertheless, laws are mostly implemented on a territorial basis, within the legal competence of national authorities.

This implies that there are limits to how effective legal regulations are in influencing behaviour outside of or between national frameworks. The international legal framework for recognition largely exists, but the

---

71. See Sjur Bergan: "A tale of two cultures in higher education policies: the rule of law or a excess of legalism?" *Journal of Studies in International Education*, volume 8, issue 2, summer 2004.

mechanisms for international enforcement are weak, and there is unlikely to be political support in the foreseeable future for such mechanisms. There is no "International Court of Recognition", nor is there an "International Recognition Police", and even the very thought seems absurd.

This is not to say that the international legal framework is worthless or ineffective. It is just to say that treating it only as a traditional legal framework is missing half the point. It is a legal framework, but at least in the vast majority of cases, its legal implementation depends on national jurisdiction, which is one of the main reasons the main provisions of the Lisbon Recognition Convention should be transposed into national law where this has not already been done. The exception is countries in which international treaties automatically become national law once the country has ratified them.

Attitudes to recognition

The second half of the point referred to above – the half that was missing – is that the international legal texts also serve as guides to good practice. In fact, there are countries – like Belgium – that for various reasons are still in the process of ratifying the Council of Europe/UNESCO Recognition Convention, but that still apply it in practice. While it is obviously desirable that all European countries ratify the Council of Europe/UNESCO Recognition Convention, as the "Bologna Ministers" committed to doing in the Berlin Communiqué, *de facto* implementation of the Convention in the absence of ratification is clearly preferable to ratification not followed by effective implementation.

What is at issue is the interpretation of legislation and recognition practice. Over the past two decades or so, there has been a very significant development from what is often referred to as "equivalence" to "recognition" – some would also say that we are now on our way towards an attitude of "acceptance". This development basically describes changing attitudes to how similar qualifications should be in order to be given recognition and, at a deeper level, a growing awareness of the important role recognition specialists have in providing a service to those who seek to move across borders without losing the true value of their qualifications.

This change in practice and attitudes implies leaving the very detailed comparison of curricula and structures behind in favour of a broader view. The world of recognition has its share of horror stories, and one of them is about a well-regarded professor who, as a member of the faculty senate at a European university a generation ago, made sure that any applicant who wanted to get recognition of a degree in a foreign language would be turned down unless the applicant had studied at least one work of literature dating from before 1700. This is a horror story for two reasons: firstly, that such a detailed – and presumably non-stated and thus informal – criterion would decide the fate of an application, and secondly that a routine application would be considered by the faculty senate rather than administratively.

Recognition, however, is not about verifying that almost all elements in the foreign qualification have a counterpart in the corresponding qualification in one's own system. After all, what is the point of studying abroad if one can study the same thing at home? Studying abroad is to a large extent about getting new perspectives and being challenged in one's traditional perceptions.

Rather, recognition is about determining whether applicants' learning achievements are such that they are likely to succeed in whatever activity they want to undertake on the basis of their qualifications, whether for further study or in the labour market. Therefore, we need to assess what applicants know and can do rather than the structures and procedures through which they have obtained their qualifications.

The development of "new-style" qualifications frameworks is a major development in this respect because they emphasise learning outcomes and relate qualifications to an overall framework that describes not only the individual qualification but also how the different qualifications within an education system interact. A national qualifications framework describes how learners may move between qualifications within a national system, whereas an overarching framework for qualifications of the European Higher Education Area will facilitate movement between systems. A working group appointed by the Bologna Follow Group and chaired by Mogens Berg has put forward a proposal for an overarching framework that was considered at a Bologna conference in Copenhagen on 13 and 14 January 2005 and that will be finalised by the end of February 2005. One important consequence for recognition is that when justifying non-recognition because of substantial differences between the home qualification and the foreign qualification for which recognition is sought, in accordance with the Council of Europe/UNESCO Recognition Convention, it will be increasingly important to do so with reference to qualifications frameworks and in particular with reference to learning outcomes and achievements.

While the development over the past couple of decades has been very positive, there is of course a caveat: it has also been very uneven. The most advanced thinking as well as practice has made great strides, but many members of the "recognition community" have not been party to this development.

Laws can be read in two ways. One can either take the view that what is not explicitly allowed cannot be done, or one can take the view that what is not explicitly forbidden is possible. In the same way, one can assess a foreign qualification by looking for differences that will justify non-recognition or one can take what Andrejs Rauhvargers has referred to as a "forgiving attitude" and look for reasons to recognise the qualification. One should also keep in mind that if it is not possible to give full recognition, the first alternative should – as is clearly stated in the Recommendation on Criteria and Procedures for the Assessment of Foreign Qualifications – not be non-recognition but partial recognition. Both attitudes can be found in Europe, as shown by a survey conducted in 2001-2002.[72]

One of the main challenges for the recognition community in establishing the European Higher Education Area by 2010 will therefore be to develop the attitudes of recognition specialists from one of detailed comparison to one of broad considerations of outcomes, from one of looking at procedures to one of looking at achievements, from one of looking for problems to one of looking for solutions. Granting fair recognition does not mean that one should recognise all qualifications regardless of their merits, but it does mean that one should look at their real merits and give them due recognition for these. If we think of recognition as a bridge that allows individuals to cross the divide from one education system to another, it is important that there be no "customs station" on the other side of the bridge that, through unreasonable procedures and unreasonable attitudes to the content of qualifications, would oblige those moving across the bridge to leave much of the real value of their qualifications behind.

Ultimately, we need to work on the assumption that recognition specialists are there to help applicants get the recognition they deserve even if they do not always know how to formulate their requests. Recognition specialists are there mainly to "protect the learner", not so much to "protect the system". The recognition specialists of 2010, even more than those of today, should be knowledgeable and broad-minded experts at the service of learners and not gatekeepers trying to keep out all but the pure.

---

72. See Sjur Bergan and Sandra Ferreira, "Implementation of the Lisbon Recognition Convention and Contributions to the Bologna Process", in Sjur Bergan (ed.): *Recognition Issues in the Bologna Process* (Strasbourg, 2003: Council of Europe Publishing), pp. 69-81.

Recognition of new forms of qualifications

Traditionally, credential evaluators assess well-documented qualifications from institutions belonging to education systems about which they have adequate information. This is, of course, an ideal situation, and it is still the most common one, but recognition specialists are increasingly faced with applications for recognition of other kinds of qualifications. Broadly speaking, these fall into two groups.

The first group is variously termed transnational education, cross-border education or borderless education.[73] Whatever their name, these are qualifications from providers that are not recognised as belonging to a national higher education system[74] or that operate outside the country in which the home institution is based. This is not a mere formality because it implies that, in most cases, the quality of the provision is not assessed and the quality of education provision is one of the main criteria in assessing a qualification. This is often true even when the home institution belongs to a national higher education system, as in many cases, there is no separate quality assessment of branch campuses or other kind of provision in foreign countries. Such provision can, however, differ significantly from that given at the home institution. It is also worth keeping in mind that the term "higher education provision" does not only cover traditional programmes given at physical institutions, but also provision through non-traditional means, such as Internet provisions.

This leads us to the second broad group, which may be termed non-traditional qualifications. This is a broad category ranging from programmes that are more or less classical in content but given through non-traditional means to informal learning and accreditation of prior learning. In this case, the common denominator is that the learning for which recognition is sought is achieved in a wide variety of ways, few of which conform to traditional conceptions of higher education, but that the results of this learning may be expressed as higher education qualifications. Expressed differently, within a coherent qualifications framework, qualifications may be obtained through different learning paths. In this context, it may be useful to keep in mind that lifelong learning may best be seen as a set of learning paths leading to qualifications that can also be obtained through more traditional learning paths.

---

73. See Jane Knight's chapter in this volume.
74. The term is borrowed from the Council of Europe/UNESCO Recognition Convention, where parties undertake, in Section VIII, to provide adequate information on institutions belonging to their higher education systems and on any programme operated by these institutions.

In most cases covered by these two broad groups, we are not talking about different qualifications but about different ways of obtaining and documenting the qualifications. This is a challenge to credential evaluators because the assessment of such qualifications is more demanding. The traditional and well-tested methods are not fully applicable. However, this development is very much in line with the increased emphasis on assessment of outcomes rather than of procedures and education systems.

"External dimension"

In "Bologna terminology", the "external dimension" is the catchword for the relationship between the European Higher Education Area and the rest of the world. I do not think the jargon is particularly appropriate, but I must also admit that I do not have a better alternative.

Whatever name we choose to give it, this is a key but so far understudied aspect of the Bologna Process.[75] In terms of recognition, the key questions are: how will qualifications from the European Higher Education Area be recognised elsewhere, how will we recognise qualifications from other parts of the world within the European Higher Education Area, and what changes in recognition practice will – or at least should – the establishment of the European Higher Education Area in 2010 bring about worldwide?

The three questions are interlinked, and the starting point is of considerable concern. The Bologna Process is complex, and we know that public perception of complex realities is often less than complete. In this case, one lingering perception is that the main point of the Bologna Process is reducing the first degree from four to three years – full stop. If this is indeed the dominant perception, I believe adequate recognition of degrees from institutions and systems in the European Higher Education Area might become difficult. That is at least the signals we get from North American recognition specialists.

A first degree of 180 ECTS credits is clearly a possibility and will most likely become common within the European Higher Education Area. Saying that a first degree has to carry a workload of 240 credits is not an option, even if some countries may choose this as their prevailing model.

---

75. An honourable exception is the conference organised by the Academic Cooperation Association in Hamburg on 18 and 19 October 2004:
http://www.aca-secretariat.be/08events/Hamburg/HamburgConferenceOverview.htm. A publication on the basis of the conference is forthcoming: Franziska Muche (ed.): *Opening up to the Wider World: The External Dimension of the Bologna Process* (ACA Papers on International Cooperation in Education, Lemmens: Bonn 2005).

Therefore, the discussion on recognition must focus on learning outcomes and qualifications frameworks not only within the Bologna Process, but also outside it. Also in a worldwide context, Europeans must argue that qualifications must be recognised on the basis of what learners know and can do rather than on the basis of a consideration of structures alone. The concept of qualifications frameworks must be developed also with a view to our relationships with higher education outside the EHEA, and Europeans must provide clear and comprehensible explanations of their respective national frameworks as well as of the overarching framework for the EHEA.

There is another aspect of the "external dimension". While it is important that the rest of the world be aware of and understand qualifications from Europe, we must avoid giving the impression that recognition is a one-way street. If we demand that others recognise our qualifications for their real value and not just on the basis of formal considerations of procedures and systems, we must be willing to do the same for qualifications from other parts of the world. To lay a better basis for this, it is important that the ENIC and NARIC Networks initiate discussions with their counterparts in other parts of the world. The UNESCO Regional Committees provide an invaluable framework for this, but few if any regions have a network of functioning national information centres that would be a fully satisfactory counterpart to the ENIC and NARIC Networks. In many countries, real information centres have yet to be established and European countries could play a role in this respect. In the framework of a MEDA project, UNESCO, the French CIEP (Centre International d'Etudes pédagogiques), the Council of Europe and some ENICs/NARICs are now engaged in establishing national information centres in four North African countries.

Information and communication

It is not difficult to make the case that information on recognition is crucial. However, the problem is often not the lack of information per se. We live in the information society, which is characterised by an overflow of information, yet at the same time there is often a lack of reliable information of good quality, and the world of recognition is no exception. The challenge is therefore to convey appropriate and understandable information to those who need it. To try to meet this challenge, the ENIC and NARIC Networks in 2004 adopted a new information strategy.[76]

---

76. This part of the chapter draws heavily on the ENIC/NARIC report on information strategies, elaborated by a working group chaired by Darius Tomaščiūnas of the Lithuanian ENIC/NARIC and of which the present author was secretary. The full report bears the reference DGIV/EDU/HE (2004) 6 rev.3.

This strategy takes as its starting point that information should:

– be meaningful to the users and respond to their needs;

– recognise that different users or user groups have different information needs and seek to provide information that is relevant to each group without overburdening them with irrelevant information;

– be accessible in terms of content, language and style (*inter alia*, avoiding unnecessary complications or specialised language);

– be accurate (*inter alia*, being factually correct and also avoiding oversimplification – implying that a balance needs to be struck between accessibility and accuracy);

– originate from – and as far as possible be provided by – the competent authority closest to the source of information (the subsidiarity principle – for example, information on a given education system should be provided by the authority competent for that system);

– be up to date;

– be easily available, in printed and/or electronic form.

Language is also an important issue in the provision of information. That information should be available in several languages is of course vital, but it is also important that, in whatever language, this information be understandable. This seems obvious and straightforward, but it can involve striking a delicate balance between being easily accessible and being accurate and complete. On the one hand, overly technical terms may not be very helpful to most target groups, but oversimplification can be equally unfortunate and may ultimately lead to misunderstanding and false hopes of recognition. Certainly, sending the complete legal texts to anyone enquiring about recognition will not be very helpful, but in some contexts it may be necessary to quote precise legal language, perhaps accompanied by an explanation of what the law actually says. Often it may also be necessary to include the necessary legal caveats to avoid having an information letter or brochure that aims to explain general rules and procedures in easily understandable terms used as evidence in a legal appeal or even a court case.

If the provision of information is to be adapted to the needs of different target groups, it is of course important that we be clear about who these groups might be, and even more important that we know who the *main* target groups are. The ENIC/NARIC information strategy considers the following as its main target groups:

- individual holders of qualifications;

- public authorities (typically – but not limited to – ministries responsible for higher education);

- quality assurance agencies;

- higher education institutions and bodies (typical examples of the latter would be rectors' conferences or similar structures and mobility and exchange agencies);

- employers;

- professional organisations;

- ENICs/NARICs.

It also suggests that there are two basic kinds of information. On the one hand, it refers to *system information* – that is, information that is relevant to a broad category of recipients and concerns the characteristics of an education system as a whole or a part of it. Typical examples would be general information on the degree structure or qualifications framework of a given country or general conditions for obtaining student support. On the other hand, the information strategy refers to *information on individual qualifications* or other kinds of information relevant to one specific individual. Examples corresponding to the ones listed for system information would be information on how a specific qualification relates to the degree system or qualifications framework of a given country, or the possible eligibility of a specific person for student support. It may of course be argued that, ultimately, this information will be the outcome of an assessment of an application, but potential applicants may seek this kind of information to assess their chances and see whether it would make sense for them to submit a formal application.

Schematically, the information strategy suggests that target groups and the kind of information to be provided match as follows:

Target group	Need system information	Needs information on individual qualifications	Receives information	Provides information
Public authorities	X	(x)	X (on foreign education)	X (on own foreign education)
Quality assurance agencies	X	(x)	X	X
HEIs and bodies	X	X	X	X
Individual holders of qualifications	(x)	X	X	(x)
Employers and professional organisations	X	X	X	X
ENICs/NARICs	X	X	X (on foreign education)	X (on own foreign education)

where X denotes that the target group in question needs or provides this type of information on a regular basis, (x) that it does so occasionally.

Even these target groups are not necessarily uniform, however, and it may be necessary to differentiate further. For example, different public authorities may require information on:

- higher education legislation – in particular the legal provision for recognition and quality assurance;
- statistics;
- qualifications framework/degree system;
- quality assurance (methods and results);
- what institutions or programmes are a part of any given higher education system;
- basic concepts and instruments for recognition;
- procedures and provision for the recognition of foreign qualifications;
- contact details and legal status of competent authorities of other countries.

Yet if one tries too hard to meet the specific needs of each subgroup, one ends up with no information strategy at all and goes back to treating information as a case-by-case need, each time with its own specificities.

The goal must be to identify a limited number of target groups that allow competent recognition authorities to provide standardised generic information that will answer most questions, while being open to address the individual enquiries that are not fully covered by the generic information.

Not least, a major but very difficult task is to raise the consciousness of students and employers about the need to verify the value of qualifications before they enrol in a study programme or hire someone with a given qualification. Surprisingly, many people seem to ask fewer questions about the study programme in which they plan to invest considerable effort and money than they would if they were buying a used car.

To seek to address this need for information, the ENIC/NARIC information strategy consists of four elements:

- a Code of Good Practice, which was formally adopted by the Networks in Strasbourg in June 2004;
- a set of frequently asked questions with generic answers;
- a list of questions prospective students and other interested parties (such as employers) should ask of education/service providers;

–   a fact sheet for national information centres, outlining information that should be readily available at national centres.

Conclusion

It is said that old soldiers never die; they just wither away. Recognition is not an old solider, and it will not wither away, nor will the need for recognition of qualifications magically disappear with the establishment of the European Higher Education Area.

The world of recognition will, however, change profoundly, or at least so I hope. Credential evaluators should spend less time assessing clear-cut cases, and this chapter will hopefully help explain why. This means that they will have more time to devote to complicated cases; the ones that truly require the sustained attention of specialists with a good knowledge of various education systems and above all with a solid knowledge of the principles of recognition and the ability to apply those principles to individual cases. This will make the work of credential evaluators much more interesting and also much more demanding. Above all, however, these developments should help those who seek recognition obtain a fair assessment of their foreign qualifications. This is crucial, both for reasons of individual justice and because their numbers are likely to increase and their backgrounds are likely to become much more diverse.

Improving the recognition system of degrees and periods of studies: conclusions and suggestions

Stephen Adam

Introduction

International conferences can lead to great progress or end in disappointing platitudes. The trick is to achieve the former and avoid the latter but this is no easy task. It is difficult to say exactly what ingredients go to make a Bologna conference a success or failure. Obviously, careful planning and good logistical organisation are important components yet despite these it is never possible to predict what precisely will emerge from any event. The most successful Bologna conferences are essentially dynamic events that reflect the interactions and opinions of those attending. They combine meticulous preparation with plenty of discussion time. The best conferences are where the practical arrangements appear smooth and non-intrusive and delegates do not feel they are being manipulated towards pre-determined recommendations.

The Riga conference on "Improving the recognition of qualifications and study credit points", organised by the Latvian Ministry of Education and Science with the help of the Council of Europe and the support of EU Socrates programme, stands out as a model example of a successful event. It combined superb organisation, well-prepared questions for discussion groups, a detailed background report and lively speakers. This conference is a positive example of what can be achieved – it generated a clear sense of progress linked with a strong agreement about the way forward embedded in a set of practical recommendations.

The main theme of the conference is a familiar one: recognition. Recognition is acknowledged to be at the heart of the Bologna Process:

> "Improving recognition of qualifications earned in one of the Bologna Process countries across all other Bologna Process countries is a necessary precondition for the successful establishment of the European Higher Education Area."[77]

---

77. Andrejs Rauhvargers, Background report for the Riga seminar, conclusion section, p. 20.

Many of the Bologna Action lines have a direct and obvious link to recognition, notably: the adoption of easily readable and comparable degrees; adoption of a system essentially based on two main cycles; promotion of mobility; promotion of European co-operation in quality assurance; promotion of the European dimension in higher education; lifelong learning; and the promotion of the attractiveness of European higher education. Without effective processes for recognition these objectives could not be achieved. This was acknowledged in the Berlin Communiqué 2003 where education ministers committed themselves to intermediate priorities for the next two years with the pledge: "...to improve the recognition of degrees and periods of study."[78]

In recent years, and certainly since the groundbreaking 1997 Council of Europe/UNESCO Convention on the Recognition of Qualifications concerning Higher Education (Lisbon Recognition Convention), there has been steady progress in the recognition field. Various international codes of practice (subsidiary texts) have served to supplement the Lisbon Recognition Convention, strengthen existing good practice, and cope with new recognition issues. Notable examples include the Council of Europe/UNESCO Recommendations on Criteria and Procedures for the Assessment of Foreign Qualifications Recognition (adopted 2001), Recommendations for the Recognition of International Access Qualifications (adopted 1999), the Code of Practice for the Provision of Transnational Education (adopted 2001), and the Recommendation on the Recognition of Joint Degrees (adopted 2004). To these advances can be added the effective work of the two European recognition networks, ENIC and NARIC, which operate in close co-operation almost as merged networks.[79] There are also the EU Directives on recognition for professional purposes. To these initiatives and organisations can be added transparency instruments such as the Diploma Supplement and the European Credit Transfer and Accumulation System (ECTS).

Collectively these initiatives are destined to play an increasingly central role in the creation of the European Higher Education Area (EHEA). Already there is evidence that synergies are emerging between the existing recognition tools that form the legal and practical recognition framework in Europe. However, we are faced with a big problem – the reality gap between having systems and processes and using them. This is borne

---

78. Berlin Communiqué: http://www.bologna-berlin2003.de
79. ENIC: Council of Europe/UNESCO European Network of Information Centres for Recognition and Mobility. NARIC: European Union Network of National Academic Information Centres. Further information can be obtained at: http://www.enic-naric.net/

out by the *Trends 2003* survey.[80] Academic and professional recognition is important as it goes to the heart of realising the free movement of citizens who are currently deterred when their qualifications are undervalued or not recognised at all. Recognition is concerned with assessing and making judgments about foreign qualifications in terms of what we are familiar with domestically. It can be reduced to the simple assessment and subsequent acknowledgement of a claim. The problem is that there is still widespread ignorance, poor practice, xenophobia and reluctance to move from viewing recognition of qualifications as a process of simply looking for exact "equivalence" rather than "fair recognition".

The Bologna Process has given a sharp boost to every aspect of the recognition field. This positive progress needs to be developed by making existing tools work better, fully implementing the Lisbon Recognition Convention and widening knowledge of good practice at all levels – local, regional, national and international. The recognition field can be likened to an iceberg. The visible parts and procedures are effective and proven to work. The problem lies with the submerged nine-tenths.

Nature and structure of the report

The purpose of the seminar was well expressed by the Latvian Minister of Education and Science, Ina Druviete, when she indicated in her opening address:

> "The goals of the Bologna Process can only be achieved, if we manage to ensure that qualifications awarded in each part of the European Higher Education Area will be recognised for both further studies and employment in the entire European Higher Education Area."

This conference was important as it marked a significant and practical step forward in achieving this. When it was planned the rationale for the conference emphasised that improving recognition of degrees and periods of studies is set as a priority for the 2003-2005 period and that recognition is set as one of the three issues for the stocktaking exercise to be undertaken for the Bergen ministerial meeting. The Berlin Communiqué recognised as a priority "furthering implementation of the Lisbon convention", "fostering recognition for further studies" and "recognition of prior learning". The conference made progress in all these areas.

This report is designed to focus on how the conference tackled these themes and what specific contributions were made over the two days of

---

80. Reichert S. and Tauch C., *Trends III: Progress Towards the European Higher Education Area*.

the event. Readers will be relieved that it does not seek to reproduce all the written or oral contributions made by every presenter – this is just not possible or useful. Indeed, the written texts are already available from the conference website.[81] What this report seeks to do is to highlight the main arguments and issues that led to a remarkable level of agreement at the end of the second day. It explores the current state of recognition and justifies where there needs to be further development in the context of the Bologna reforms.

This report closely follows the sequence of sessions in the original programme except that it integrates its comments on the various individual presentations on the main themes with the working group discussions on the same topics. This is sensible in that there is a logical progression to the conference that moved from exploration of the background situation, through themed presentations, working group discussions and reports, stakeholder panels, and views on recognition in 2010. It was this rich diet of presentation, discussion and debate that led to the positive set of conclusions and recommendations. Above all, this report seeks to explore the development of the main argument and issues that surfaced during the event.

The conference background report (Andrejs Rauhvargers)

The conference immeasurably benefited from a purpose-written background report by Andrejs Rauhvargers. His report, with a similar title to the conference, "Improving the recognition of qualifications and study credit points", provided a comprehensive overview of not only the current state of recognition matters, but also the key issues and problems to be faced now.

Both in his report and particularly in his subsequent presentation at the conference he gave us a timely reminder of the multiple facets to recognition. It is worth repeating key parts of his message:

---

81. The seven main themes (in order of presentation) were: Jindra Divis (NUFFIC), "Recognition and quality assurance"; Julia González (University of Deusto, Bilbao), "Developments along subject lines and their impact on recognition"; Dirk Haaksman (NUFFIC), "Recognition and the labour market"; Norman Sharp (UK QAA), "Recognising learning outcomes"; Stephen Adam (University of Westminster), "Qualifications frameworks and recognition"; Volker Gehmlich (Fachhochschule Osnabrück), "Recognition of credit points – achievements and problems"; and Jane Knight (University of Toronto), "Programmes, providers and accreditors on the move: implications for recognition". Presentation papers can be downloaded from:
http://www.aic.lv/rigaseminar/documents/index.htm.

- recognition is important for higher education institutions (HEIs) in terms of the institution securing recognition for itself both nationally and internationally;

- the recognition of actual higher education programmes is another dimension as institutional recognition does not necessarily imply that all a recognised institution's qualifications are nationally or internationally recognised;

- recognition of an individual qualification nationally and internationally as valid for further studies and employment purposes raises the crucial dimension of the level of recognition given – whether full, partial or no recognition is forthcoming.

The background conference report also details the international legal framework for recognition, the work of the European recognition networks (ENIC and NARIC), and the necessary links between quality assurance, learning outcomes, transnational education and recognition. It is not the place or purpose of this conference report to repeat these aspects, suffice it to say that they came up directly and indirectly throughout the conference.

In his conference presentation Andrejs Rauhvargers provided an entertaining "masterclass" detailing the links between recognition and such diverse elements as transnational education, learning outcomes, legal frameworks, quality assurance, new/old degrees, the Tuning project, lifelong learning, joint degrees and transparency tools. Few who were fortunate to attend the conference will forget the complex PowerPoint "spider diagram" he created that charted the numerous interactions between the different elements of higher education and recognition.

The main messages of Andrejs Rauhvargers' report and presentation were that:

- ratification of the Lisbon Recognition Convention was not enough if the principles of the convention were not transposed to national legislation and institutional practice;

- one of the biggest challenges was to raise institutional awareness (a recurring theme of the conference) and knowledge of their responsibilities under the Convention;

- bottlenecks exist between the proper recognition of lifelong learning and inflexible national education structures;

- we need to improve recognition practice on the ground. There are sufficient legal and practical recognition tools in existence – the problem lies in ensuring their use;

- those involved in recognition must adopt a forgiving attitude, reflecting the progression from seeking absolute "equivalence" to "fair recognition".

An "outside" view of recognition – the stakeholder panel

It is difficult adequately to do justice to the rich set of contributions made by the stakeholder panel. The panel were asked to reflect upon and provide an "outside" view of recognition.[82] In so doing a number of interesting dimensions and insights were identified including:

- we must not forget "periods of study" when we consider recognition matters. This aspect can become lost in the effort to concentrate on qualifications;

- all those involved in higher education are experiencing a (painful?) transition period as the waves of Bologna-inspired reforms combine with other domestic educational reforms. Periods of change do cause uncertainty and even a backlash effect. We all need to be sensitive to such issues and need to persuade stakeholders of the positive benefits to citizens and employers;

- it is important that the tendency to over-regulation is avoided. There are sufficient legal and practical tools already in existence. It must not be forgotten that reform, particularly for HEI, comes at a cost;

- institutional autonomy is very important and furthermore is implied by many new Bologna developments. In terms of recognition we must not forget that most recognition decisions are taken by institutions. Furthermore, in many states new relationships between competent authorities and newly autonomous HEIs are being developed. This building of new relationships is a sensitive and difficult area that has not sufficiently been explored;

- there are serious "information overload" problems facing citizens, who are often confronted by complex, unfiltered information that

---

82. The stakeholder panel included: Students: Predrag Lazetic, ESIB, Brussels; Credential evaluators working at HEIs: Hans Knutell – University of Uppsala, Sweden; HEI leadership: Janis Vetra, Riga Stradiņa University, Latvia; Ministries of Education: Marie-Anne Persoons, Flemish Ministry of Education, Belgium; reflection from outside Europe: Timothy Thompson, University of Pittsburgh, USA. It was chaired by Sjur Bergan, Council of Europe.

makes decision making difficult. A solution to this is the "empowerment" of learners where they are given guidance on what sort of critical questions they need to ask about institutional providers, their qualifications and the subsequent national and international academic and professional recognition;

–　it is increasingly vital that those concerned with the Bologna Process reforms give more thought to how the "new Bologna degrees" are regarded outside the EHEA. Timothy Thompson gave a salutary reminder of the importance of how others (non-Bologna countries) regard us. There are dangers if Bologna degrees erroneously become associated with reduced standards and the worth of our degrees is questioned.

Furthering implementation of the Lisbon Convention at national level

Working group one had the task of exploring "furthering implementation of the Lisbon Recognition Convention at national level".[83] Perhaps the most significant point to arise was the strong conviction that when the Lisbon Recognition Convention is ratified the job is not done but just started! Too often, following ratification, there is little practical change in the behaviour of credential evaluators. The Convention is commonly regarded as "soft law" even when enacted into national legislation as there is no effective appeals mechanism. The reality is that, in practice, the "burden of proof" is not switched from the student to the assessing institution. There is no change in mentality, procedure or outcome. Despite some good progress much remains to be done in order to reverse attitudes from looking for reasons to deny recognition to positively seeking to give recognition.

The real challenge that faces us is to achieve the long-term goal: to encourage the mutual trust that exists between HEIs within a state and to replicate this trust at the level of the European Higher Education Area. This would obviously involve the thorough embedding of the principles of the Lisbon Recognition Convention within national law and subsequently in the processes of all European HEIs. It must not be overlooked that most recognition decisions are taken at the level of institutions. It is good practice to decentralise the recognition decision power at the level of HEIs and to centralise the recognition decision power for academic recognition of final degrees for professional purposes.

---

83. Chair: Rolf Lofstad, Norwegian ENIC/NARIC, Oslo; Rapporteur: Erwin Malfroy, Flemish ENIC/NARIC, Brussels; Resource persons: Štepanka Skuhrová, Czech ENIC/NARIC, Darius Tamoşiunas, Lithuanian ENIC/NARIC.

The implementation of the Lisbon Recognition Convention is too often confined to a top-down exercise that has left it isolated and extraneous. Steps must be taken to secure its practical implementation at a local level, along with the other Bologna Process innovations.

Development in the recognition of degrees and study credit points

Working group two examined the "development in the recognition of degrees and study credit points".[84] In this session concerns were voiced again about potential misunderstandings of Bologna reforms associated with "outside" perceptions of new first cycle degrees of three years' duration. Timothy Thompson (University of Pittsburgh) and Stephen Hunt (US Network of Education Information, US Department of Education) raised this issue – the latter making his intervention by transatlantic phone call. Part of the problem is that countries outside the Bologna Process perceive Europe as a set of piecemeal individual education systems and not a single entity. This is not surprising; Europe will not be regarded as a linked set of integrated educational frameworks until the EHEA becomes a reality. It is important that, in the interim period, negative preconceptions about "Bologna degrees" are not allowed to develop. This danger is compounded by the fact that different countries are naturally at different stages of progress with their Bologna reforms. Furthermore, it needs to be explained that European education systems will remain diverse in the sense of the content, style, detailed features and regulation of their education systems. The commonality between them will come through shared understanding of standards and the use of common ways to express levels and describe qualifications. It is clear that the European Credit Transfer and Accumulation Systems (ECTS) will play an important role in the development of the EHEA. This will entail European HEIs expressing their qualifications, courses and modules in terms of learning outcomes and levels – such a transformation in approach will take much time and a huge staff development effort.

Recognition of learning outcomes

Working group three focused on the "recognition of learning outcomes".[85] There was unanimous agreement about significant advantages

---

84. Chair: Gunnar Vaht, Estonian ENIC/NARIC, Tallinn, President of the ENIC Network; Rapporteur: Gabriel Vignoli, Italian Erasmus Mundus Agency, Rome; Resource persons: Timothy Thompson, University of Pittsburgh, USA, Volker Gehmlich, Fachhochschule Osnabrück, Germany.
85. Chair: Norman Sharp, Quality Assurance Agency, Glasgow, Scotland; Rapporteur: Sjur Bergan, Council of Europe, Strasbourg; Resource persons: Dirk Haaksman, NUFFIC, the Netherlands; Tatjana Koķe, University of Latvia, Riga; Jane Knight, University of Toronto, Canada.

of adopting "learning outcomes" as an integral part of a modern approach to formulate and implement higher education policy. Such an approach has implications at the local, national and international levels.[86] Learning outcomes are precise statements of what a learner is expected to know, understand and/or do as a result of a learning experience. Learning outcomes need to be clearly stated and are intimately linked to the construction and expression of the curricula, the process of learning, the learning delivery mode and the assessment of learning. The introduction and expression of modules and qualifications in terms of learning outcomes will certainly require enormous staff development at all levels (including the Bologna Promoters).

The adoption of a learning outcomes approach has obvious advantages for those involved with credential evaluation. The focus of credential evaluation is shifting from an emphasis on input characteristics (workload, level of resources, and so on) towards more precise output-focused learning outcome (what a successful student can do). This output focus also has benefits for the recognition of transnational education, joint degrees and lifelong learning. The new emphasis on what the holder of a qualification can do is beneficial for learners and employers who get more information on what skills and competencies qualifications provide. When modules or course units are expressed in learning outcomes it is much easier to make accurate judgments because there is more transparency to help the evaluation process. Learning outcomes improve the transparency of qualifications and make credential evaluation easier and judgments more accurate. In effect they provide a common language/methodological approach. They also facilitate the recognition of work-based learning (WBL) (through the use of APEL techniques) and lifelong learning. Perhaps their strongest merit is that they simplify our understanding of the curriculum as well as the development of common subject reference points (typified by the Tuning project). ECTS based on learning outcomes becomes more effective.

Despite these considerable advantages it must be acknowledged that there are problems associated with the design, definition and assessment of learning outcomes. Academic staff can easily resent such innovations. Learning outcomes must be written with great subtlety and sensitivity to avoid the reduction of learning to training. These are issues that all the stakeholders in the education systems must engage with as a matter of importance.

---

86. Explored at the UK Bologna Conference on "Using learning outcomes", Heriot-Watt University, Edinburgh, 1-2 July 2004.

Using the results of quality assurance for improving recognition

Working group four explored "using the results of quality assurance for improving recognition".[87] The direct link between quality assurance and recognition is obvious. There needs to be confidence between countries despite them having different quality assurance arrangements. Without such confidence international judgments about qualifications and the institutions from which they originate become suspect as the qualifications may not be of an appropriate standard or even fit for their stated purposes.

The cross-border recognition of higher education qualifications/institutions is the most important objective of quality assurance in the international setting. Reciprocal confidence in each other's quality assurance systems contributes to the culture of mutual trust in the European Higher Education Area. The development of qualifications frameworks will aid international recognition and lessen concerns about quality by placing qualifications in a clear national and international context.

A strong concern was expressed about the insufficient level of co-operation between the recognition and quality assurance sectors. It is clear that without closer co-operation between these bodies international recognition suffers. The Bologna Process must involve the full exploitation of national and international expertise and all stakeholders should be consulted. It is regrettable if ENIC and NARIC Networks are not fully consulted at the international level regarding quality assurance matters. The development of closer links between those responsible for quality assurance and recognition is paramount but it must not be imagined that effective quality assurance systems will ever abolish the need for recognition. Recognition is an issue that concerns the individual. The gaining of effective recognition in a host country's educational or employment system is not just about general declarations but the provision of advice, support and practical results.

A further concern was voiced associated with the dangers of non-traditional providers being left outside the remit of quality assurance agencies. Transnational education providers should have the possibility of gaining recognition within national frameworks. This is important for several reasons. In many cases such providers remain outside national education

---

87. Chair: Séamus Puirséil, Higher Education and Training Awards Council, Dublin; Rapporteur: Carita Blomqvist, Finnish ENIC/NARIC, Helsinki; Resource persons: Marlies Leegwater, Dutch Ministry of Education, The Hague; Julia González, University of Deusto, Bilbao.

systems, often subject to little or no quality assurance. If transn. education providers are not given the opportunity to apply for ofi. recognition for themselves and their qualifications they will rema. unregulated and "consumer protection" will be absent. Transnational education, both imported and exported education, is a significant feature of international education and should not be ignored. Obviously, any official recognition process by a competent authority must be rigorous and ongoing. There is a need to encourage good transnational providers and discourage "degree mills".

Impact of emerging qualifications frameworks on recognition

Working group five looked at "the impact of emerging qualifications frameworks on recognition".[88] The discussions centred on the Bologna Follow-up Group (BFUG) qualifications frameworks working group outline proposals contained in the report for the Bologna seminar on "A Framework for Qualifications of the European Higher Education Area".[89] There was clear agreement on the vital importance of "new-style" national qualifications frameworks and the need for an overarching European framework for qualifications.

"New-style" output-focused national frameworks employ "workload, level, learning outcomes, competencies and profile" plus credits, and are very different from traditional input-focused approaches used to place and explain qualifications. Furthermore, frameworks provide more explicit and precise information in their qualifications descriptors and their reference to other external reference points. It is these features that will impact most on the recognition field.

It is no coincidence that in the recognition area there is a trend towards emphasising the fair recognition of qualifications based on what a person knows and is able to do rather than on the formal procedures that have led to qualifications. Furthermore, in an effort to promote more accurate judgments of qualifications, it is apparent that detailed comparisons of the formal aspects of individual qualifications (curriculum content, status of institution, recommended textbooks, duration/contact hours, access requirements, and so on) give a less accurate basis for evaluation. It is more helpful when qualifications are situated within national

---

88. Chair: Mogens Berg, Danish Ministry of Education, Copenhagen; Rapporteur: Eva Gönczi, Hungarian Ministry of Education, Budapest; Resource persons: Anne-Katherine Mandrup, Danish ENIC/NARIC, Copenhagen; Gerard Madill, Universities Scotland, Edinburgh.
89. Danish Bologna Seminar, Copenhagen Business School, 13-14 January 2005. The background conference report is available at http://www.bologna-bergen2005.no/.

qualifications frameworks that are characterised by a clear description of learning outcomes, supplemented by a consideration of level, workload and profile. A strong advantage of qualifications frameworks is that they can, for the purposes of comparison, provide a more accurate basis and explanation of qualifications.

It was emphasised that the overarching framework for qualifications is not regulatory. It is not about creating convergence but understanding and clearly expressing the differences between qualifications and different European higher education systems. There was a strong opinion that qualification frameworks represent a powerful boost for the Lisbon Recognition Convention. Henceforth, it would be natural to express "substantial differences" with reference to qualifications frameworks and in particular learning outcomes.

The international recognition of qualifications builds on transparency. A framework, which provides a common understanding of the outcomes represented by a qualification rather than a mere assertion of comparability will greatly enhance the usefulness of qualifications across the European Higher Education Area. A variety of purposes are associated with the international recognition of qualifications including employment, access to further qualifications, exemption from parts of studies, access to continuing education, and enhancing mobility. The development of a common overarching framework through the collaborative efforts of stakeholders across Europe will enhance the other actions being taken to improve recognition for these purposes.

The international mobility of learners depends on the recognition of their prior learning and qualifications gained. Learners moving between qualifications or cycles require recognition in order to access more advanced programmes. Students moving within their studies, and their advisers, can benefit from the clarity that may be provided through the specification of the level and nature of the study programmes. Learners can have greater confidence that the outcomes of study abroad will contribute to the qualification sought in their home country. A framework will be of particular help in supporting the development and recognition of joint degrees from more than one country.

It is clear that qualifications frameworks are being promoted in order to have a beneficial effect on transparency, recognition and mobility. They are likely to have a large impact on existing recognition tools and practices. If they do not, the very rationale for their existence is undermined. A useful way to identify their precise potential benefits is to explore them in terms of a number of key questions associated with their use.

The potential benefits to recognition from qualifications frameworks can be summarised as follows. Qualifications frameworks:

– improve the transparency of qualifications, make credential evaluation easier (for HEIs and other stakeholders) and judgments more accurate;

– act as a common language/methodological approach that internationally can improve recognition and understanding between educational systems;

– facilitate the recognition of APEL and lifelong learning between states;

– simplify our understanding and improve the expression of the curriculum between countries through the use of common reference points;

– facilitate the application of the Lisbon Recognition Convention and the Code of Good Practice in the Provision of Transnational Education;

– ease the pressure of work on the ENIC-NARIC Network;

– make ECTS based on learning outcomes and levels more effective;

– allow HEIs and credential evaluators to move away from imprecise measurement indicators that focus on formal procedures (admissions criteria, length of studies, qualification titles, years/hours of study undertaken) to focus on the results of student learning, and to move from input measurements to output/outcome measurements.

The introduction of qualifications frameworks represents both a challenge and the opportunity to improve recognition. In theory, they have the potential to improve the clarity, accuracy and fairness of the recognition process. They can provide reference points against which clear decisions can be made. Increased transparency between national systems can lead to more trust and confidence. However, it will also provide real evidence of major differences in outcomes that may cause "zones of distrust". This is not necessarily a negative point as substantial differences between qualifications need to be acknowledged. There are a number of long-standing recognition problems that appear to defy resolution; frameworks and their associated methodological tools may help. The application of the Lisbon Recognition Convention should be made more effective. Qualifications frameworks could help to support a more constructive approach towards transnational education providers.

Finally, a number of interesting questions were raised. Firstly, about the impact of non-recognition when it takes place where a qualifications framework exists – what will be the process of arbitration and appeal? The second area of concern was the relationship of the EHEA qualifications frameworks developments in relation to the European Commission's plans to develop a credit-based European framework for lifelong learning.

For the reason identified above it was suggested that there is a need for intensive national and international dialogue to share good practice associated with the introduction of qualifications frameworks and their impact on recognition processes and issues.

Recognition 2010 – vision of the future

The panel who considered what recognition might be like in 2010 faced a difficult task attempting to peer like clairvoyants into the future.[90] It was emphasised that recognition would be firmly based on the expression and evaluation of learning outcomes. It was suggested that that qualifications will become more diverse and earned through a process of lifelong learning and offered via multiple learning pathways and modes. Credit will play a major part in developments. In the future no legal obstacles should exist in the recognition of transnational education, which will be regulated, and learners will be clearly informed about the quality and worth of such providers through the substantial developments in information provision and strategies. Students and citizens will be more empowered so they have clear information before making choices about study programmes and institutions.[91] There is likely to be more focus on recognition for the purpose of employment, in particular for the non-regulated part of the labour market.

Finally, it was suggested that we are at a crossroads and need to decide how to negotiate our future direction with care.

Conclusions

It can be seen from the snapshot of the debates and contributions described in this report that a number of recurring themes emerge, notably that many good tools for recognition already exist; the real question concerns their practical implementation. New elements to be added to the existing tools are qualifications frameworks and learning outcomes. The conference engendered a robust sense of purpose and a clear call for some practical action. Recognition is not an area where we can rest on our lau-

---

90. Sjur Bergan, Council of Europe, Strasbourg; Germain Dondelinger, Ministry of Education, Luxembourg and incoming Chair of the Bologna Follow-up Group (spring 2005); Ruard Wallis de Vries, European Commission, Brussels; Gunnar Vaht, President of the ENIC Network, Estonia.
91. The new ENIC-NARIC information strategy, adopted in 2004, will play a major role in student empowerment.

rels and complacently regard it as substantially resolved. Amongst the conference delegates were some of the foremost European experts in the recognition field and they identified the need for further action. There is always a danger for any conference that it might produce few ideas, simply reprise familiar comments and lead to marginal changes. In the event nothing was further from the truth. The Riga event has unequivocally identified what must be done to complete the contribution of recognition to the creation of the EHEA. The conference marked an important step forward and this can be seen from the overall conclusions summarised below:

–   There is no reason for complacency. Existing recognition tools, improvements in quality assurance and the development of qualifications frameworks will not alone solve all recognition problems. They must be fully implemented but even then the dream of automatic recognition is only obtainable in very limited circumstances.

–   The conference delegates highlighted the intimate links between the work of quality assurance and recognition experts. This needs to be acknowledged by all concerned and to lead to better co-operation between the two areas.

–   The development of national qualifications frameworks and the overarching framework for qualifications for the EHEA can immeasurably strengthen existing recognition tools. However, the latter must not be viewed (or implemented) as a device to limit diversity or restrict innovation. They involve a convergence in methodological approach but not qualification content, delivery or learning outcomes.

–   We need to recognise the huge importance, and potential contribution to recognition, of learning outcomes, but enthusiasm for them must be tempered with some understanding of the enormity of the task of introducing them.

–   More efforts need to be made to eradicate false expectations created through meaningless declarations of formal recognition that fail to lead to employment or admission to/exemption from study.

–   We must find ways to make the Lisbon Recognition Convention more effective. It needs to be fully plugged into national legislation, institutional practice and national quality assurance systems.

–   We need to tackle some of the recognition bottlenecks. This will involve modernisation of existing educational systems so that they can seamlessly integrate all forms of education, including lifelong learning, in the award of domestic higher education qualifications.

- ECTS credits "in the real world" must be expressed in terms of learning outcomes and levels. Credits must be the subject of "fair recognition" giving proper recognition based on learning outcomes, particularly as they are important for the recognition of work-based learning and the use of Accreditation of Prior Experiential Learning (APEL) techniques.

- Delegates supported the adoption of a mature approach towards good transnational education (TNE) provision by making it eligible for official recognition (both TNE providers and qualifications). There also needs to be a more co-ordinated effort to marginalise degree mills and "illegal" institutions. Qualifications frameworks should help solve some of the problems in devising effective ways to accredit/recognise TNE providers.

- The stakeholder panel reminded us that there are dangers associated with the Bologna Process. In particular, how Bologna degrees are viewed globally is of vital importance. The reduction in the length of European first-cycle degrees must be accompanied by the creation of suitable qualifications frameworks based on explicit external reference points (such as qualification descriptors, level, level indicators, workload, quality, learning outcomes and profile). It is imperative that the nature, purpose and quality of the Bologna reforms are communicated to the rest of the world.

- Existing recognition tools alone (Lisbon Recognition Convention, Diploma Supplement, codes of practice, ECTS, and so on) will not solve all recognition problems. There will always be a major role for individual recognition in order to position the foreign qualification properly in the host country's educational or employment system.

A sense of optimism and purpose developed during the conference. The end product of the event is the set of recommendations outlined below. Earlier there was mention of the "recognition iceberg" which represents the hidden expanses of recognition problems we still need to resolve. It may be deeply unfashionable, in this age of concerns about global warming, but we really do have to melt the "recognition iceberg" and resolve the prejudice, ignorance, xenophobia, inertia, poor practice, confusing qualification titles, unclear educational systems, imprecise terminology, etc. The collective set of existing recognition tools aided by new qualifications frameworks, learning outcomes and a fully implemented Lisbon Recognition Convention are collectively capable of dissolving those problems previously regarded as insoluble.

Improving the recognition system of degrees and study credit points in the European Higher Education Area

Conference recommendations

Ministers in Bergen are urged to:

1. Amend national legislation to incorporate the principles of the Council of Europe/UNESCO Convention on the Recognition of Qualifications concerning Higher Education in the European Region (1997 Lisbon Recognition Convention) and adopt effective measures to ensure their practical implementation at all appropriate levels.

2. Recognise that reaching the ambitious goals of the Bologna Process and the European Council's Lisbon Strategy requires defining "recognition" as positioning a holder of a foreign qualification in the host country's education or employment system rather than a formal act of acknowledging his or her qualification, and therefore to:

   • emphasise the benefits of "new-style" national qualifications frameworks and endorse the creation of the overarching framework of qualifications for the EHEA on the grounds of their positive contribution to international recognition, mobility and transparency;

   • promote an intensive national and international dialogue, informed by ENICs and NARICs, to exchange good practice.

3. As a matter of urgency, launch a campaign to convey accurate and pertinent information on the Bologna Process to other parts of the world.

At the level of ENIC and NARIC Networks it is recommended that:

4. The existing co-operation between recognition and quality assurance networks should be further strengthened. It needs to be acknowledged that recognition and quality assurance are intimately related.

5. The networks further explore ways in which the emerging national and European overarching qualifications frameworks and usage of learning outcomes can be applied for improving recognition practices, including the recognition of lifelong learning and other non-

traditional qualifications, and how they relate to the legal framework of the Lisbon Recognition Convention.

6. The networks take an active part in the information campaign on the Bologna Process in the wider world, using their long-standing contacts and information exchange channels.

At the national level it is recommended that:

7. Effective measures are taken in respect of non-traditional providers of education to offer them access to state recognition procedures and ongoing quality assurance monitoring.

8. The vital contribution of learning outcomes to recognition in higher education and lifelong learning is acknowledged and a strategy for their implementation is developed. The development of learning outcomes should take into account the four main purposes of higher education:

    • preparation for the labour market;

    • preparation for life as an active citizen;

    • personal development;

    • the development and maintenance of a broad, advanced knowledge base.

9. Steps are taken to monitor the implementation of the Lisbon Recognition Convention, with a view to encouraging fair and equal treatment of applicants within countries.

At the level of higher education institutions it is recommended that:

10. HEIs draw more on the experience and knowledge of ENICs and NARICs to support and inform recognition decisions taken at institutional level.

11. HEIs take steps to develop institutional recognition policies and practices and to disseminate information on the legal framework for recognition and best practice at the level of faculties and individual study programmes.

12. HEI leaderships, together with EUA, EURASHE, ENICs and NARICs, develop a co-ordinated strategy in order to play an effective role in implementing the principles of fair recognition embodied in the Lisbon Recognition Convention and reflected in the Bologna Process.

List of contributors

Editors

Sjur Bergan

Head of the Department of Higher Education and History Teaching, Council of Europe, and a member of the Bologna Follow-up Group and Board. Secretary to the Council of Europe's Steering Committee for Higher Education and Research.

Andrejs Rauhvargers

Professor of Education at the University of Latvia and Secretary General of the Latvian Rectors' Conference. President of the Lisbon Recognition Convention Committee and former president of the ENIC Network.

Authors

Stephen Adam

Principal lecturer and leader of the undergraduate politics area in the Department of Social and Political Studies at the University of Westminster. Author/Rapporteur of a number of research projects, studies and conferences related to the Bologna Process.

Jindra Divis

Head of the Dutch ENIC/NARIC. Former President of the ENIC Network; member of the NARIC Advisory Board.

Volker Gemlich

Professor of Economics at the Fachhochschule Osnabrück. Has played a prominent role in the development and dissemination of the European Credit Transfer System (ECTS) and in the Tuning Project.

Julia González

Vice-Rector for International Relations, Universidad de Deusto. Co-ordinator of the Tuning Project, with Robert Wagenaar.

E. Stephen Hunt

United States Department of Education. Director of the US ENIC; author of numerous publications.

Jane Knight

Adjunct Professor, Comparative International Development Education Centre, Ontario Institute for Studies in Education, University of Toronto, and the author of numerous papers on borderless higher education.

Norman Sharp

Director of the Scottish Office of the Quality Assurance Agency for Higher Education.

Timothy S. Thompson

Assistant Director for Admissions in the Office of International Services, University of Pittsburgh. Chair of the National Council on the Evaluation of Foreign Academic Credentials.

Robert Wagenaar

Professor of History, Rijksuniversiteit Groningen. Co-ordinator of the Tuning Project, with Julia González.

Sales agents for publications of the Council of Europe
Agents de vente des publications du Conseil de l'Europe

BELGIUM/BELGIQUE
La Librairie Européenne -
The European Bookshop
Rue de l'Orme, 1
B-1040 BRUXELLES
Tel.: +32 (0)2 231 04 35
Fax: +32 (0)2 735 08 60
E-mail: order@libeurop.be
http://www.libeurop.be

Jean De Lannoy
Avenue du Roi 202 Koningslaan
B-1190 BRUXELLES
Tel.: +32 (0)2 538 43 08
Fax: +32 (0)2 538 08 41
E-mail: jean.de.lannoy@dl-servi.com
http://www.jean-de-lannoy.be

CANADA
Renouf Publishing Co. Ltd.
1-5369 Canotek Road
OTTAWA, Ontario K1J 9J3, Canada
Tel.: +1 613 745 2665
Fax: +1 613 745 7660
Toll-Free Tel.: (866) 767-6766
E-mail: order.dept@renoufbooks.com
http://www.renoufbooks.com

CZECH REPUBLIC/
RÉPUBLIQUE TCHÈQUE
Suweco CZ, s.r.o.
Klecakova 347
CZ-180 21 PRAHA 9
Tel.: +420 2 424 59 204
Fax: +420 2 848 21 646
E-mail: import@suweco.cz
http://www.suweco.cz

DENMARK/DANEMARK
GAD
Vimmelskaftet 32
DK-1161 KØBENHAVN K
Tel.: +45 77 66 60 00
Fax: +45 77 66 60 01
E-mail: gad@gad.dk
http://www.gad.dk

FINLAND/FINLANDE
Akateeminen Kirjakauppa
PO Box 128
Keskuskatu 1
FIN-00100 HELSINKI
Tel.: +358 (0)9 121 4430
Fax: +358 (0)9 121 4242
E-mail: akatilaus@akateeminen.com
http://www.akateeminen.com

FRANCE
La Documentation française
(diffusion/distribution France entière)
124, rue Henri Barbusse
F-93308 AUBERVILLIERS CEDEX
Tél.: +33 (0)1 40 15 70 00
Fax: +33 (0)1 40 15 68 00
E-mail: commande@ladocumentationfrancaise.fr
http://www.ladocumentationfrancaise.fr

Librairie Kléber
1 rue des Francs Bourgeois
F-67000 STRASBOURG
Tel.: +33 (0)3 88 15 78 88
Fax: +33 (0)3 88 15 78 80
E-mail: francois.wolfermann@librairie-kleber.fr
http://www.librairie-kleber.com

GERMANY/ALLEMAGNE
AUSTRIA/AUTRICHE
UNO Verlag GmbH
August-Bebel-Allee 6
D-53175 BONN
Tel.: +49 (0)228 94 90 20
Fax: +49 (0)228 94 90 222
E-mail: bestellung@uno-verlag.de
http://www.uno-verlag.de

GREECE/GRÈCE
Librairie Kauffmann s.a.
Stadiou 28
GR-105 64 ATHINAI
Tel.: +30 210 32 55 321
Fax.: +30 210 32 30 320
E-mail: ord@otenet.gr
http://www.kauffmann.gr

HUNGARY/HONGRIE
Euro Info Service
Pannónia u. 58.
PF. 1039
H - 1136 BUDAPEST
Tel.: +36 1 329 2170
Fax: +36 1 349 2053
E-mail: euroinfo@euroinfo.hu
http://www.euroinfo.hu

ITALY/ITALIE
Licosa SpA
Via Duca di Calabria, 1/1
I-50125 FIRENZE
Tel.: +39 0556 483215
Fax: +39 0556 41257
E-mail: licosa@licosa.com
http://www.licosa.com

MEXICO/MEXIQUE
Mundi-Prensa México, S.A. De C.V.
Río Pánuco, 141 Delegación Cuauhtémoc
06500 MÉXICO, D.F.
Tel.: +52 (01)55 55 33 56 58
Fax: +52 (01)55 55 14 67 99
E-mail: mundiprensa@mundiprensa.com.mx
http://www.mundiprensa.com.mx

NETHERLANDS/PAYS-BAS
Roodveldt Import BV
Nieuwe Hemweg 50
1013 CX Amsterdam
The Netherlands
Tel.: + 31 20 622 8035
Fax.: + 31 20 625 5493
Website: www.publidis.org
Email: orders@publidis.org

NORWAY/NORVÈGE
Akademika
Postboks 84 Blindern
N-0314 OSLO
Tel.: +47 2 218 8100
Fax: +47 2 218 8103
E-mail: support@akademika.no
http://www.akademika.no

POLAND/POLOGNE
Ars Polona JSC
25 Obroncow Street
PL-03-933 WARSZAWA
Tel.: +48 (0)22 509 86 00
Fax: +48 (0)22 509 86 10
E-mail: arspolona@arspolona.com.pl
http://www.arspolona.com.pl

PORTUGAL
Livraria Portugal
(Dias & Andrade, Lda.)
Rua do Carmo, 70
P-1200-094 LISBOA
Tel.: +351 21 347 42 82 / 85
Fax: +351 21 347 02 64
E-mail: info@livrariaportugal.pt
http://www.livrariaportugal.pt

RUSSIAN FEDERATION/
FÉDÉRATION DE RUSSIE
Ves Mir
9a, Kolpacnhyi per.
RU-101000 MOSCOW
Tel.: +7 (8)495 623 6839
Fax: +7 (8)495 625 4269
E-mail: orders@vesmirbooks.ru
http://www.vesmirbooks.ru

SPAIN/ESPAGNE
Mundi-Prensa Libros, s.a.
Castelló, 37
E-28001 MADRID
Tel.: +34 914 36 37 00
Fax: +34 915 75 39 98
E-mail: libreria@mundiprensa.es
http://www.mundiprensa.com

SWITZERLAND/SUISSE
Planetis Sàrl
16 chemin des pins
CH-1273 Arzier
Tel.: +41 22 366 51 77
Fax: +41 22 366 51 78
E-mail: info@planetis.ch

UNITED KINGDOM/ROYAUME-UNI
The Stationery Office Ltd
PO Box 29
GB-NORWICH NR3 1GN
Tel.: +44 (0)870 600 5522
Fax: +44 (0)870 600 5533
E-mail: book.enquiries@tso.co.uk
http://www.tsoshop.co.uk

UNITED STATES and CANADA/
ÉTATS-UNIS et CANADA
Manhattan Publishing Company
468 Albany Post Road
CROTTON-ON-HUDSON, NY 10520, USA
Tel.: +1 914 271 5194
Fax: +1 914 271 5856
E-mail: Info@manhattanpublishing.com
http://www.manhattanpublishing.com

Council of Europe Publishing/Editions du Conseil de l'Europe
F-67075 Strasbourg Cedex
Tel.: +33 (0)3 88 41 25 81 – Fax: +33 (0)3 88 41 39 10 – E-mail: publishing@coe.int – Website: http://book.coe.int